CW01509837

TOUCHING THE BRAKE
— a Tour Guide's Journey to South Africa

*How I Stopped Chasing Money
and Followed My Dream*

Nick Bailey

authorHOUSE®

AuthorHouse™
1663 Liberty Drive, Suite 200
Bloomington, IN 47403
www.authorhouse.com
Phone: 1-800-839-8640

First published by AuthorHouse 5/21/2009

ISBN: 978-1-4389-4343-5 (sc)

Printed in the United States of America
Bloomington, Indiana

This book is printed on acid-free paper.

To the memory of Sybil Stephenson
(1915-2008)

Contents

Acknowledgements

I thank all those unknown friends who at some point in recent years, having enjoyed my e-mails sent during my various travels, suggested I should turn them into a book.

I am indebted to June Wyles for her constant support and ideas and for allowing me the time to write this book.

I thank Mindy Gibbons-Klein, 'The Book Midwife', for providing the inspiration to start, and who set me on the right track. Also Lesley Morrissey, and particularly Fiona Cowan from 'The Book Cooks' for her editing, suggestions and guidance throughout the book for many months.

Janine Bloomberg's view from the South African perspective has been very welcome.

I thank Vicky Billingham who was the first to enjoy my book and her comments were priceless.

Siggy Thetard was invaluable in ensuring the text was correct in the final review.

The publishers Authorhouse provided an excellent service in getting the book designed and onto the shelves.

Introduction

Have you ever met a person who struck you as amazing? Who appeared to have such a fantastic life that you couldn't help but envy them?

I can see it now: 'Wow!' you thought. 'I wish I could be like that, but...' and then you were brought back to reality, your admiration trailing off into a sea of excuses.

You probably do have genuine reasons for being *ordinary* rather than *amazing*. You have to pay the mortgage, or perhaps you don't want to leave behind your friends and family. But the truth is, if you really want to do something different, you can. You just need the right mindset. I did it. And so, therefore, can you.

This is the story of how I changed my life around, despite suffering from a lot of the same obstacles that everyone else has. We've all read books about how a person achieved an amazing life after hitting rock-bottom in some way: their choice was 'sink or swim'. In my case, I did it because I wanted to make a change — although I didn't recognise it at the time and would not have believed then what might actually happen in my future.

My upbringing was unspectacular. I grew up a normal lad, in the country. My father was a policeman, a man of great standing in his community and holding strong ethical values for which I will always be grateful. Like many boys of that time, I was brought up to be 'seen and not heard'. I failed my Eleven-Plus exam, a disaster for me. Later, tired of studying after my A-Levels, I didn't go to university either. Instead, I wanted to get a job before they became in short supply.

So there I was, an ordinary boy growing up in the depths of the English countryside … and here I am today, being a tour guide in South Africa. I spend six months in Cape Town and the other half of the year in the UK, enjoying the British summer.

I feel as if I have the best, most satisfying and enjoyable life imaginable. But when I look deeper into how I got here, I'm surprised by what I find.

How did a little country lad end up here, 8,500 kilometres from home on the African continent? Throughout this book, I will share with you how I made that transition. And along the way, I'll share some of my favourite stories and characters from the tours that I guide.

In each chapter, I'll reflect on how my life changed, bit by bit, gradually bringing you up to date. Some were surprisingly small, but the accumulation of even those minor adjustments would make a huge difference in building my philosophy, attitude and outlook on life.

When I look back at how I used to be, I find it difficult to remember how it felt to be that person.

I hope you will find this book inspiring. Even if you remember only one special thing after reading it, I will feel it's been worth all the hard work and soul searching that I have put into writing it.

To make it easier for you, at the end of each

chapter you will find some lessons learnt. It will be possible for you to dip in and out of chapters, and pick up on the lessons I have learnt at each stage, which may well relate to something in your life, if that's how you prefer to read this book.

If you have never been to South Africa you may read this book and gain useful background information on such a beautiful and varied country.

Like me, you've probably said to yourself many times: 'I wish I'd known then what I know now!' Well, now you can learn from my experiences and save yourself valuable time.

And remember, it is never too late to learn!

South Africa

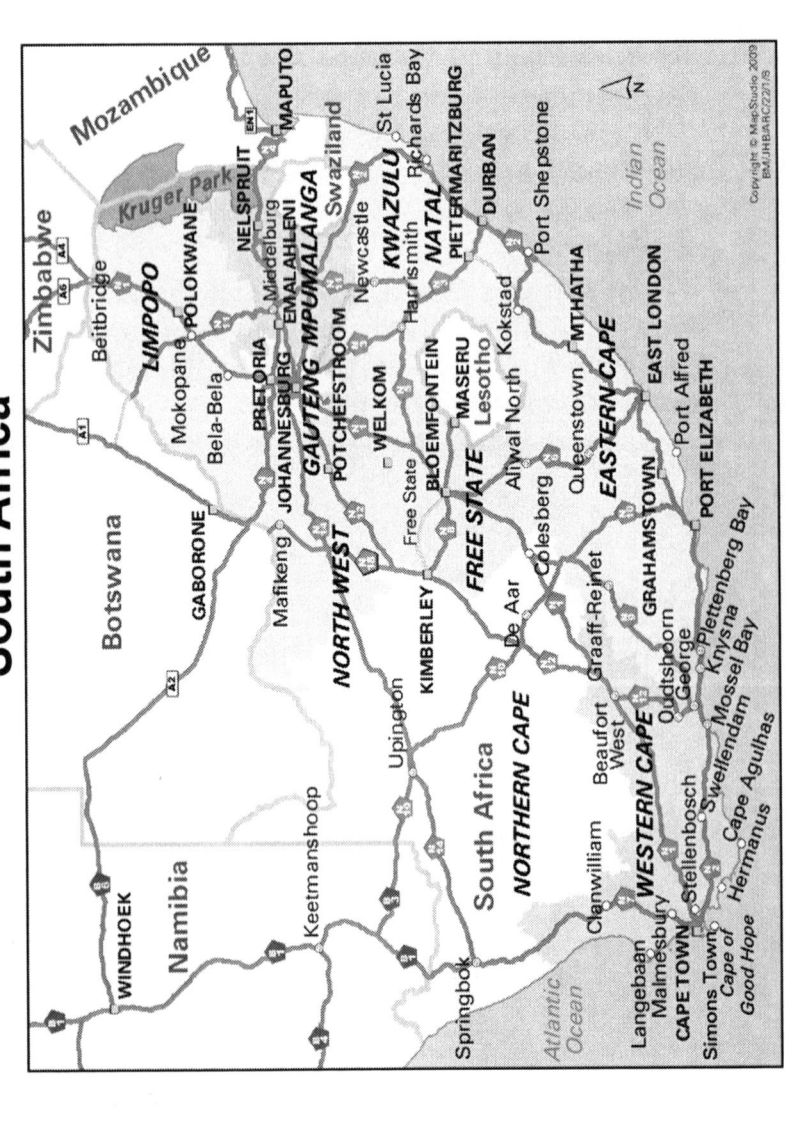

Chapter 1
The Peninsula Tour

In my experience, anyone who visits South Africa is stunned by its beauty. Cape Town is the jewel in its crown.

I always say you need at least three holidays to see South Africa properly: Cape Town and the Garden Route; Mpumalanga Province in the north including the Kruger National Park; and KwaZulu-Natal with its mind-blowing diversity.

The weather is consistent, so you can plan ahead without worrying about unexpected rain. Imagine hardly ever having to carry a raincoat, and going around in a t-shirt and shorts all the time!

It's a privilege, to be able to feast my eyes on this beautiful land every day if I want to, while I guide tourists around it. Sometimes I have to pinch myself.

This season alone, I have guided the Peninsula tour more than 40 times — and I never tire of it. The people make each tour unique.

My job involves driving a tour company minibus around the streets of Cape Town, picking up tourists and showing them the coast, explaining what they are seeing.

The tour starts just as we leave Cape Town. We see the beach road as we pass through Sea Point, the locals exercising along the promenade. South Africans enjoy outdoor activities, taking advantage of the benign weather. In the early morning and late afternoon you can see them taking in the fresh air, jogging, cycling, walking the dog.

Often I break the ice with a story about the open air swimming pool that used to be right on the beach at Sea Point. It was frequented by men bathing naked. A lady made an official complaint that she was tired of seeing so many men's bottoms. The Police visited her apartment to investigate, and found that to see anything at all they had to stand on a chair, on a table, with binoculars!

Life on the beach

Cape Town's main beaches are at Clifton. The old beach in Cape Town, where ships used to anchor, disappeared in the 1930s when the area was reclaimed for the dockland and foreshore development.

All the beaches at Clifton are generally sheltered from the south-easterly wind that blows throughout the summer months. This wind is called the 'Cape Doctor' because it blows away the cobwebs and pollution. It can be very strong, and is said to have toppled double-decker buses.

The widest beach on the peninsula is North Beach in Noordhoek, which means 'North Corner' in Afrikaans. The rip tides and back currents make it less attractive for swimming but ideal for walking and horse riding. There are a number of stables nearby.

At the end of the beach is a black blob — all that remains of the *Kakapo*. In May 1900 this ship was on her maiden voyage from Southampton to New Zealand. She was fully laden with coal, having refuelled in Cape Town, when just out of port she was hit by a north-westerly storm. For some reason the captain turned into the bay and hit the beach.

The ship itself was not badly damaged — but, being full of coal, all efforts to salvage the ship failed and it remained there to rot. The children enjoyed catching fish which got stranded in the wreck when the tide went out. In 1969 the *Kakapo* was used as a set in David Lean's film *Ryan's Daughter*. The sides were dressed up and a papier-mâché funnel added. Afterwards it was all left to the mercy of the elements.

Fynbos and the Cape Floral Kingdom

Walking along this coastline, you notice the dry, heath-like landscape.

The Cape Floral Kingdom is unique because of its vegetation. 'Fynbos' means 'fine bush' in Afrikaans, and consists of small-leafed shrub which grows in poor soil. It is found all over the Cape peninsula, along the Garden Route, some areas along the East coast, some patches in the north of the country, just across the South African border — and almost nowhere else in the world. This small area has among the highest level of endemic species in the world.

Fynbos comprises three main species: protea, erica and restio. The most striking are the proteas, with the huge King Protea being the national flower of South Africa.

The Fynbos area gets its diversity from its many different soils including infertile sands, granite, chalk and limestone. The large variation in the amount and timing of rainfall also has an effect. Over millions of years the peninsula has escaped devastating droughts and ice ages, allowing the vegetation to develop and diversify freely.

Heads in the sand

This harsh environment suits ostriches, which live off the fynbos vegetation. The ostrich is one of my favourite animals, often seen in the wild on the peninsula, or down near the water's edge. You can also see them at the Cape Point Ostrich Show Farm, near the entrance to the nature reserve.

Ostriches were bred for their feathers in the late 19th century when ladies of high society wore feathers in their hats and clothes. The industry went into decline in the years leading up to the start of the First World War, but not before many 'feather palaces' were built on the profits from the feather industry.

Nowadays, ostriches are farmed for their meat, eggs and leather. The meat is tender and very low in cholesterol. The leather is made into products such as handbags, purses and wallets and has a distinctive mark where the feather was attached. Empty ostrich eggs can be sold either plain white or as an impressive brightly hand-painted ornament.

Oudtshoorn, along the Garden Route, is known as the ostrich feather capital of the world. Until I visited Cango Ostrich Farm, I hadn't realised that ostriches have a liking for shiny items such as watch straps and cameras. I was quite taken by an albino pair and started videoing one of them. Suddenly, out of sight from my right, its mate lunged for my camera. I nearly jumped out of my skin when his beak hit the camera — luckily without damaging it.

Also at this show farm, I kissed an ostrich. Well, I held some food between my lips and a tame ostrich took it from me. Not for the faint hearted, but a good trick for amusing tourists.

See tourist — think food!

When I am guiding, we nearly always meet the baboons. We see Chacma baboons in the road and have to stop because they are blocking our path. There they will play, groom each other or suck up some small item from the road surface. When the babies are around the baboons are far more interesting, with a mother carrying at least one youngster hanging on her underside. Others prove their agility by climbing up a lamp post or the adjacent rock face as if they have sticky feet.

There are many troupes of baboons in the area. Especially when carrying babies they look cute — but they are an aggressive animal, particularly the alpha male which has huge incisor teeth and strength three times that of a man. Whilst they eat the fruit from the local fynbos vegetation, they have learned to associate tourists with food. It's easier to harass tourists than to feed naturally. It doesn't help that occasionally a tourist will foolishly feed a baboon!

I know of one tour guide who had her jacket ripped off and torn to shreds. In another attack, a baby was bitten by a baboon. I advise my tourists to take great care and to keep windows closed when there are baboons about. And I insist that they don't carry food.

In March 2007, during a scheduled tour, we arrived at the Cape Point car park to find a large number of baboons hanging around and no national park monitors, a situation I had not seen before. Again, I warned everybody not to bring food back to the bus. One lady thought that the sandwich she had just bought didn't count, as it was encased in plastic. The nearest baboon had other ideas and snatched it out of her hand. Hearing her shriek, I looked round just in time to see the baboon walk off with her lunch. I had to keep the baboons at bay while her husband bought more sandwiches and smuggled them aboard.

However, by taking the right precautions there is no reason why people shouldn't have an enjoyable experience with the baboons.

On one tour in April 2007, there was a moment that I would *not* class as an enjoyable experience. I was guiding a Chinese family on a private tour and we stopped for lunch at a seafood restaurant. We could see there were baboons in the area, and the waiters were keeping an eye on them.

We were tucking into some bread while our main course was being prepared, when a baboon jumped onto the table and stole all the bread he could get his hands on. I had just buttered my own slice when this large male baboon came from behind me and sat on my corner of the table. Initially, I was a little scared. This wild baboon towered over me at the table. I was also concerned for my clients, having seen the potential danger of these animals, and urged them to leave the baboon alone and to leave the bread too. He took my slice and then grabbed all the other slices, before delicately crossing the table and disappearing.

Apparently, he is known to like bread and is not a threat when any other foods are around.

The restaurant staff were very apologetic and quickly replaced our bread and plates.

As the family's daughter remarked afterwards: 'It was amazing how he walked across the table without touching a glass or smashing anything!'

The Cape Peninsula troups are the only protected baboons of the species in Africa. Despite this local people shoot them if they become a nuisance. Visitors feeding them result in signing their death warrant, as they then become dependent on tourists for food. Eventually they become too aggressive and have to be shot.

A local lady called Jenni started organising the monitoring of these baboons. Initially, using only public donations, she was able to employ people from the local township of Masiphumelele to monitor the baboons and keep them away from tourists. Since she started in 1999, Jenny and her team have reduced baboon incidents with their human neighbours by 80 per cent.

The baboons at Cape Point have developed a liking for sand hoppers and shellfish. They can be seen scavenging for them at low tide, which is unusual in primates accustomed to feeding on fruits, roots, bulbs, insects and scorpions.

Meeting of the oceans

Many people choose to visit Cape Point because it is known as the place where two oceans meet: the Atlantic and the Indian. Geographically, where the two oceans meet is the southernmost point, Cape Agulhas, 170 kilometres east of Cape Point.

The Cape of Good Hope, next door to Cape Point, is the most south-westerly point on the African continent. Everybody likes to have their picture taken beside the sign recording the longitude and latitude of the area.

The currents have an effect on the meeting of the two oceans, somewhere between Cape Agulhas and Cape Point. The Agulhas current travels south from Mozambique, bringing warm water, which is why the beaches of Durban are so popular. The Benguela current spins off the Antarctic and travels north, bringing cold water past Cape Town and up the West coast.

Fishing is affected, too. The warm currents bring large varieties of tropical fish to the Durban waters, whilst the cold current contains something like eleven times more nitrogen than the other current, bringing plankton and krill. These microscopic creatures provide food for huge quantities of deep sea fish such as sardines and pilchards. There are fewer varieties here which explains why most fishing ports are on the west coast.

The currents also have an impact on the region's weather. The warm current evaporates under the sun and the vapour condenses on the mountain range all along the coast. This provides rain, making the vegetation particularly green.

That's why this part of the coast is known as the Garden Route.

Off the western coast the water is colder and little of the water evaporates. The region is relatively dry, turning into semi-arid desert. Further north is the full blown 'Namib' desert of Namibia.

Once, I was guiding friends on a short holiday visiting Cape Town. It was the first time after taking my exams that I had acted as a guide. They asked me to suggest where to drive. I agreed to guide them for free, as it would be useful experience for me, and in return they bought me lunch.

At Cape Point, my friends and I walked up the hill to the old lighthouse to enjoy the panorama from the end of the peninsula, despite the windy weather. As we took in the view, I could see a hawk in the near distance at eye level, out at sea. It had obviously seen some prey on the ground, and was hovering. The hawk appeared not to move at all — all the more amazing on such a gusty day.

On another Cape Point tour, there was an abundance of striped mice. I had seen two of the cute little mammals earlier, as I stretched my legs up to the lighthouse and back. Back on the minibus, one lady told me she had been looking at a mouse on the step one minute — the next, a hawk appeared, grabbed it in its claws and flew off with it. Although she was clearly shaken, her remark amused me: 'I was the last person to see that mouse alive!'

The Cape of Good Hope is a spot I love. When I am not busy taking group photographs for visitors, as every good tour guide should, I stand and look out to sea, drinking in the fresh air with its flavours of salt and seaweed. I watch the waves breaking on the beach just in front of me, and the Cape cormorants diving into the sea for fish.

On days when the winds are strong, the view is spectacular. The bigger waves at the headland buffet the rocks, and plumes of white water are fired up towards the sky. When winds are light, I like to step away from the tourists and spend a while in my own little world, savouring the moment. At such times, I feel grateful to be able to see this wonderful part of the world on a regular basis. Many visitors manage only fifteen minutes in a whole lifetime.

Without the silver paper

Half an hour's drive from Cape Point is a runaway favourite with all the tourists: the penguin colony.

These cute little birds nest on the beach at Boulders Bay, one of three land based colonies around the coast. They were once called jackass penguins because of the donkey-like braying noise they make. However, to avoid confusion with a South American penguin also known as the jackass, in South Africa it has reverted back to its original name of the African penguin.

The colony at Boulders Beach started in 1982 with the arrival of two breeding pairs, and quickly increased to around 3,000. Most of South Africa's 24 penguin colonies are on islands off the Western Cape. Boulders is one of the few colonies expanding in numbers — other colonies are reducing. No-one knows exactly why. Predators could be to blame, and of course some penguins will have vacated other islands to move to Boulders Beach.

From a boardwalk, you can watch the penguins standing in the sun on the beach, or digging holes in the sand to build their nests. They are comical creatures, like cartoon waiters in frock-coats.

In the breeding season, between March and May, the mother will generally have two chicks. Feeding is shared by both parents, with one going fishing for a day or two while the other stands guard at the nest. The returning parent then feeds the chick regurgitated fish — mainly pilchards, anchovies and a little squid.

Have you ever wondered why penguins are black and white? The white blends into the light, when you look at it from below, and the black on top of the bird blends in with the blackness of the deep, seen from above.

Penguins hunt in packs. They will circle a large shoal of fish swimming in ever decreasing circles to concentrate their prey. The fish get dazzled by the black and white colours flashing past, and other penguins will then attack the shoal and feed. This exercise will be repeated so that other penguins can take their turn to feed.

A DVD on sale in the area tells the story of the city penguins. *City Slickers* is an amusing film about penguins that wander around the streets of nearby Simon's Town and live in people's garden sheds. They get up to mischief, such as hiding in houses where the doors have been left open and parading down the streets obstructing passing traffic. They were a novelty when they first arrived on the mainland. Then they became a nuisance, digging up gardens for their nests. Eventually the locals saw their potential as a tourist attraction, and now the penguins are tolerated, living side by side with the human population.

Some South African guides tell this British joke: why don't polar bears eat penguins? Because they can't get the silver paper off! Tourists from other countries don't know about the biscuit, in the UK, called a penguin that used to be wrapped in silver paper.

THE EARLY YEARS

When I look back at the person I used to be, I am amazed that today I'm confident enough to guide a day tour in an exotic land far away. As a child I was very shy; kind and helpful, but afraid of the big wide world.

I grew up in a small village called Stoke St Michael in Somerset, England. Our postal address was given as 'near Bath' but our nearest town was Shepton Mallet where we had to go for everything from weekly shopping, to the dentist, to attend Scouts and for the swimming pool.

Our village was in a valley in the Mendip Hills, so any of the roads out of Stoke started with a difficult uphill climb on a bicycle. In later years I wouldn't miss those hills.

I have always been a country boy and loved the farms. My brother had a friend who lived on a farm and occasionally I'd be invited to join them playing in the many barns, and making 'houses' with hay bales.

I adore the smells of the countryside and the peace and quiet. Even now, when I pass a farm and get a whiff of animal, it takes me straight back to those childhood days.

As kids, we would spend hours outside playing on our bikes, or swinging from a tree on a rope. When the snow arrived we would get our sledges out and whoosh down the hill in the field adjacent to our house. Our mother wouldn't put the fire on until very late in the afternoon so we had to keep ourselves busy and warm until then.

Once, with the help of a friend, I tried to make a raft from old oil barrels and planks of wood to sail on a local reservoir. I learned that you can't just nail wood into metal, and shouldn't have been surprised when we lifted the raft and the wood parted company from the barrels. I succeeded in standing on a nail as we turned the top of the raft over, nails facing up, and had to be taken to hospital by my friend's parents for an anti-tetanus jab.

Later, I made a go-kart from old pram wheels and planks of wood, in which I raced around my parent's house, taking turns with my siblings to push. We would put obstacles like the dustbin in the way to make the course more difficult. Thank goodness our mother didn't appear at the wrong time or she would have been run over!

I remember walking through fields of yellow cowslips and seeing delicate snowdrops dotted along the banks of the river where we were playing. Each summer I would watch with great excitement as the large combine harvesters appeared in the fields.

The older boys in the village were taken on by the local farmer to help with collecting the bales of hay, and they appeared to be paid with cider at the local pub. I longed for the day when I would be old enough and big enough to join them and help lift one of the huge bales onto the tractor trailer — and to drink cider too.

I never realised my goal because we moved out of the area before that time came.

At the age of 11 the family moved to Weston-super-Mare. I had failed my 'Eleven Plus' exam and my parents thought my younger brother and sister would have a better chance in a large town.

This turned out to be true as we all had greater opportunities in Weston. Whilst I missed the countryside, there were more things to do in the town, and now we had the beach life and could swim every day if we wished. The school was bigger with more subject choices, and I had more friends than before.

When I was thirteen, my father found me a part-time job in a car accessory shop, saying: 'If you want to go on the school trip to Switzerland you'll have to save up for it.'

My first responsibility was to tidy up in the back of the shop. Gradually I progressed to learning how to do simple repairs, changing tyres and making number plates. I loved it, and barely noticed how much I was learning about cars.

Now and then, the boss would have to pop out for something and I'd be expected to look after the shop for a while. I was petrified that a customer would ask me a question I couldn't answer. If anyone did, I would have to ask the customer to wait until the boss came back, and then hang around, embarrassed, while he talked to him or her.

After one of these awkward episodes, I had an idea. The next time I was in the shop alone, I strolled around the shelves and read all the labels on the containers.

While I was doing this, a customer came in saying: 'My car's bodywork has gone dull. What product will bring the shine back?' Luckily, I had just read exactly that product description on a red jar, so I advised him to use that product.

The customer picked up the red jar and read the label himself.

'You're right!' he said, smiling. 'Thanks, I'll buy it.'

My real progress in life started at that moment.

Later, I went to work for Uncle Richard in his cycle shop. I would watch and learn while my uncle and his manager, Ian, would use their expertise to sell the bicycles. In time, I too had the opportunity to sell to a customer. I found that I would use the best techniques I had learnt, and mould them into my own style. This became a valuable lesson for me: why waste time learning something from scratch by yourself, when you can use the best of ideas from others? There is nothing wrong with copying.

I left school at eighteen, having got my A-Levels out of the way. I was tired of studying and never wanted to do that again. When, suddenly, I found myself attending college three nights a week, working towards my professional exams, I realised I might well have been able to get into university after all.

Leaving home was another turning point.

I had accepted a job as a trainee quantity surveyor with a company called Costain Construction, based in London. Not knowing where I would be living or how long I would be away, I packed a suitcase for two weeks and my Dad took me to the station to catch the London train.

Starting at Costain that Monday morning, I was sent to one of the regional offices in South West London, and then down to a construction site in Southampton. That evening I called my parents.

'How are you, son? Where are you staying?'

'In digs in Southampton.'

'But I'm *sure* that was the London train I put you on…?'

There I was, a shy person in a strange part of the country, with nothing but strangers around me. I was now working for a living, a new concept for me. I was attending college three nights and one day per week, again surrounded by new people. This was the first test of my ability to fit in and adapt; a survival technique that has served me well ever since.

Lodging with a nearby family, the Bournes, became the only stable part of this revolution in my life. It felt like home from home. Ivy took on the role of 'mum', doing my washing and ironing, making sandwiches for my lunch, and often warming up the evening meal for me when I came home late.

I didn't feel lonely in those days. But I was *alone*.

The Bournes needed their privacy, and I didn't want to get under their feet. Even so, there was only so much time I could spend up in my room. The only other option was to travel home regularly.

You can imagine how hard it was in those early months, to leave my parents' house early on Sunday evening, for the two-hour drive to Southampton. My father's well-intended best wishes and reminders about driving carefully only prolonged the moment of parting and made me feel worse.

In fact, once I was on the road again I felt more positive and cheerful.

When I wasn't with my parents, I would go out for a drink with a friend from college. Steve was a member of the sailing club at Hythe, and at weekends we would meet up with his sailing friends in the New Forest. Later, I crewed in the winter races for Mike, another member of the club. Sailing was not my passion — but I enjoyed the fresh air and sunshine, as well as the friendship for a while.

The night before the last race of the season, there had been a party. On the morning of the race, when I should have been at the sailing club, ready to race, I lay awake in my sleeping bag on Steve's floor feeling too hung-over to move.

With a huge effort I dragged myself out of bed and into my car. The drive to Hythe didn't take long on a Sunday morning. When I arrived, everyone else seemed to be running late as well. In the event, it was too windy for safety and eventually the race was abandoned. Not soon enough! Several times, I was swept overboard and plunged into the freezing water, saved only by the 'trapeze', the wires I was attached to as I hung over the side of the boat.

On the plus side, it was a great hangover cure!

I can't remember a time when I have been colder. Immediately after the race I had no feeling in my fingers which made undoing knots impossible.

By this time I had my own car, and more independence. I started to strike a balance, between seeing my parents only every *second* weekend, and staying in Southampton the other weekend to start building a proper life there. Like many a young lad, I would tinker happily with my car, or join Ivy's husband Jeff watching Southampton when they played a home game at 'The Del'.

Since my twenties I'd been bored with package holidays and longed to do something more exotic. Resorts such as the Costa Brava, Majorca, the Greek Islands and Turkey were pleasant enough but they had one thing in common: too many British tourists speaking English, usually loudly.

A breath of fresh air came when my then-girlfriend Karen and I caught a flight to Bangkok. Friends thought we were very adventurous to book just the flight and the first night's accommodation. The thrill of the unknown appealed to us; clearly, our friends were more conservative travellers.

I shall never forget that wonderful holiday. Looking back, it was the first time I had ever gone off-road to experience the local people in the rural areas.

After this first taste of exotic holidays, a friend called Valerie introduced me to adventure holidays. Looking at the brochures they seemed expensive, compared with what I would have paid for a holiday up until that point anyway. On closer inspection, however, I realised how much more I'd get out of the trip — and decided to investigate further by trying one.

Over the next twelve years I travelled to more than eighteen countries. I feasted my eyes on such glorious sights as the Taj Mahal and the home of the Terracotta Warriors. I had unforgettable experiences like walking through the rugged Everest valley. This was the start of my interest in travelling, and it led me on to my current path.

On those early journeys I met countless interesting people. Travelling takes me out of the narrow field of people I mix with in my normal working and social life, and exposes me to a much wider range of individuals from all walks of life.

I know I am lucky to be able to afford these trips, and I am thankful for the opportunity to enjoy these extraordinary experiences. Once a few travellers get together, they can talk forever about their journeys. It took me a while to learn not to strive to prove I was better than anyone else, or that I had travelled more extensively, or that I had even better stories than theirs. Travellers' tales can become a very competitive exercise, far from being the relaxing evening it's supposed to be.

During my thirties my travelling was limited to a summer holiday each year, lasting two and later three weeks. Sometimes, I would have a second, short holiday too. At work, I gained a reputation for taking exotic holidays. People I didn't see from one year to the next would ask: 'Where have you been *this* time?' and each holiday I described seemed more colourful than the one before, in their eyes.

Friends at home looked forward to seeing my photo albums. One of them told me: 'I enjoy your photographs because they always come with such fascinating stories.'

Here are a few of my less likely holiday memories: I have slid on my bum down the icy slopes of Vulcan Villarrica in Chile; suffered altitude sickness on the Inca Trail to Machu Pichu in Peru and in the Everest valley of Nepal; crawled through the Cu Chi tunnels left by the Viet Cong in Vietnam; swum with seals in the Galapagos Islands; dived with thresher sharks in the Philippines and great white sharks near Cape Town; been naked in a lift in Kyoto, Japan; lived with a local family in Quito, Ecuador; skydived over Queenstown, New Zealand and abseiled from Table Mountain in Cape Town; spent six days on the Trans-Siberian Express; slept in a beehive hut in Swaziland and on a bed of straw on a farm in rural China.

You can see that travelling has been important to me for a long time, and it's no surprise to find travelling so dominant in my life today. And yet I could happily hang up my travelling boots right now if my life were to take a different turn.

I have never been the type of person who doesn't want to come back to work. I would always pack such a lot into my trips that the return home was a welcome rest. These days I do take it a little more slowly. And I go back to work eagerly, motivated to pay for the next trip!

The one thing that I *don't* look forward to as my trip comes to an end is travelling to work every day. It takes a week and a half of commuting to get myself back into work mode. By about Wednesday of the second week I tend to crash out at home in the evenings; a measure of just how much energy commuting requires.

At weekends, I need lie-ins on Saturday and Sunday to recover properly from the week, before starting all over again on Monday. I used to be in a state of mental fuzz on Saturdays, while I recovered from the punishing week of commuting and work. Commuting by train is not as tiring as driving, and I recover more quickly from that, yet it is always more frustrating.

The one thing I told myself every year, and the thing that prevented me from continuing indefinitely down this path, was: *I will not endure commuting day after day any longer.* This has motivated me to find something better.

Now, when I am guiding, all that travelling experience pays off because I can relate to the foreign travellers I meet. Whenever I collect a party from their hotel, I ask them where they are from. More often than not, I have visited their own country, and we strike up a conversation about their homeland. Being able to say that *I* enjoyed my visit to *their* country puts them at ease. Then I introduce them to the other visitors, particularly if they are also from the same or neighbouring countries, leaving them to get acquainted while I finish my pick-ups and find the road out of Cape Town.

Back to the Peninsula Tour — and a dog's life

I love the story of the 'stray' dog from Simon's Town. You will find it hard to believe but it's all true.

The Dutch East India Company started the refreshment station at the Cape in 1652. In the early years in winter they lost many ships to the North-westerly gales at Table Bay. These ships were often fully laden with goods and treasures from the Spice Islands and the Far East, ready to sail to Europe. There was no harbour at that time, just an anchorage. Many ships were lost — some 23 ships in one night in May 1865.

Because of this, Simon van der Stel, the first governor of the Dutch East India Company, travelled overland to the other side of the peninsula in search of a sheltered winter anchorage. He found what he was looking for and that town became known as Simon's Town.

It was later established as a naval base by the British during their occupation and became a favourite stop-over for sailors. In 1957, the base was handed over to the South African Navy.

During the Second World War, a dog roamed Simon's Town. He was no ordinary Great Dane, being massive in height and breadth of chest. Unsuspecting sailors thought they had met a lion, because of his size and his ear-piercing 'lion-like' bark. When he stood on his hind legs and put his huge paws on a man's shoulders he would be a menacing threat to anyone.

33

Nuisance was no mutt, however, being born of parents with excellent pedigree and having a registered pedigree himself. Little is known of his early life until he was bought by Mr Benjamin Chaney who worked for the United Services Institute at Simon's Town. The Institute provided welfare and comfort to servicemen and women at the naval base. The dog had such freedom to wander the area that he might have been taken for a stray.

He had a preference for the branches of the Royal Navy whose uniforms were known as 'square rig' — that is, bell-bottomed trousers and a tight jumper — nobody knows why. He didn't care for any other uniform, such as the 'fore-and-aft rig' of other branches of the Royal Navy, and almost without exception ignored senior officers, chief petty officers and petty officers. He disliked females unless they were Great Danes too.

He was an exceptionally intelligent dog and travelled by train to and from Cape Town with navy ratings during their shore leave. He often ensured that ratings got back to shore base on time, and would be seen tugging at the sleeve of a sleeping sailor after the train had returned to Simon's Town.

Nuisance would hang around the base, sleeping next to the bed of a rating in 'square rig' or dozing in the corridor when people had work to do. Not knowing his previous name, everyone called him 'Nuisance'.

New recruits would watch fascinated at the barrack door as Nuisance bounded out to do his morning ablution. He would pick a place far away from the barracks and scratch a hole. Having done what a dog's gotta do, he would step forward and kick dirt with his back legs until the hole was covered. Then he would wipe his paws on the grass and lick them clean before re-entering the barracks.

Nuisance also liked trains. Being so huge, he took up three seats. Navy ratings had so much respect for the dog that they would rather stand in the crowded corridor than ask Nuisance to make room for them.

But the rail authorities didn't share their enthusiasm. As they saw it, a dog was travelling on trains without a ticket and terrorising railway staff. They wanted Nuisance to be put down. The sailors were obviously upset by this threat, and Nuisance was also loved by the senior officers by this time, even though he still ignored them.

By now, Nuisance was a legend in the Navy and with citizens of the Cape too. There was an outcry from thousands of people at the thought of what the rail authorities might do. As a last resort, the Admiralty decided to make him one of their own.

In August 1939, Nuisance was taken to the senior officer to complete the dog's papers. 'What's his name, boy?' the senior officer asked the man who had brought him. 'Well, he's … um … um … well, just Nuisance.'

So it was that the dog became known as Able Seaman Just Nuisance. He was the only dog ever to be officially listed in the ranks of the Royal Navy, in peace or war time. By Admiralty orders he was officially excused from wearing his hat at any time — the only member of the civil service to be so excused, from Admiral of the Fleet down to the lowest rank of ordinary seaman. Nuisance would wear his hat around his neck and was given a free pass on the railway, by means of a metal disc attached to his collar.

Nuisance was seconded to *HMS Afrikander*, a shore-based naval establishment at Simon's Town. He later bunked at Froggy Pond, five miles away. On his certificate of service his trade or occupation was recorded as 'bone crusher' and his religious denomination as 'scrounger'.

Nuisance enjoyed his beer and was often seen in one or other of his favourite ale houses. Once, his commander had to send instructions to the landlords to restrict the dog's consumption to three quarts of ale, after Nuisance had once come home rather worse for wear and wobbly on his legs.

Nuisance had a friend, a bulldog called Ajax. On the first occasion he joined Nuisance on a trip to Simon's Town, Nuisance jumped aboard easily but Ajax, with his short legs, simply could not leap high enough to enter the carriage. Nuisance, seeing the distress of his friend, jumped back on to the platform and gently edged his big nose under the mutt's body and flipped him into the train with such force that Ajax cart-wheeled into the back of the carriage, landing on his back. Nuisance calmly jumped aboard again, took his friend by the scruff of the neck and lifted him on to all fours.

The second incident is even more preposterous. Some of the ratings frequented a café known as Mayor's Garden which many servicemen liked, owing to the cheap prices and excellent food. The café was serviced by cooks and waitresses who were unpaid volunteers. Nuisance was there with many of his *oppos*. At one end of the dining room was a stage with a settee on it and after his meal Nuisance settled down on the settee. There was a man on stage too playing dance tunes on an old piano, and some of the waitresses would offer themselves as a partner to any serviceman who requested a dance. On this particular evening Nuisance must have felt a bit lively. He sprang down from the settee and wandered over to a young lady. The pianist was playing a waltz and as Nuisance approached this girl, she jokingly asked if he wanted a dance.

She was more surprised than anyone when Nuisance's tail wagged furiously in reply. To everyone's amazement, Nuisance reared up on his hind legs, delicately put his paws on the girl's shoulders and danced in perfect time to the music. Many years later, the lady wrote in the local paper that being only five foot two, the dog towered over her, but they went off in correct time — 1, 2, 3 … 1, 2, 3 — and he even guided her by putting pressure on a shoulder to indicate which way he wanted to turn. What a beautiful memory that lady has.

The dog was involved in a few incidents in his short years and escaped serious injury many times. Alas, in his seventh year he was seen jumping from a moving bus and lorry and injured his back legs on both occasions. His health deteriorated after that, and he never recovered. He was put to sleep, ironically on the day of his seventh birthday, 1st April 1944.

As befitting a member of the Royal Navy, Nuisance was buried with full naval honours. There is now a grave on the hill overlooking Simon's Town harbour, and a memorial in the town to this legend of a dog.

In Terrance Sisson's book *Just Nuisance AB — His Full Story*, he writes: 'In my opinion [a medal] was no more than Able Seaman Nuisance deserved, not for gallantry against the enemy, but for comradeship, loyalty, assistance and the great affection he had for his oppos.'

One of the great botanical gardens of the world

A lovely place to finish off a day tour of the peninsula is the Kirstenbosch National Botanical Gardens, located directly behind Table Mountain. After spending a busy day in traffic and winding my way through crowds of people, the green peaceful gardens are a balm to the soul before returning to Cape Town to drop off my clients.

Originally owned by the Dutch East India Company, the gardens were started in 1657. Jan van Riebeeck arranged for a group of shipwrecked refugees to build a wild almond hedge to outline the boundary of the Dutch outpost. Wild almond makes a very dense hedge and it provided a natural barrier to cattle thieves.

The gardens came into private hands, the last owner being Cecil John Rhodes who purchased them in 1895. Upon his death in 1902, they were bequeathed to the people of South Africa. Kirstenbosch became a botanical garden in 1913, dedicated to the cultivation and study of the indigenous plants of South Africa.

Consisting of many themed gardens, Kirstenbosch covers some 528 hectares (more than 1,300 acres) on the eastern slopes of Table Mountain. These include the Protea Garden, the Erica Garden, the Fynbos Walk and, especially for the blind and partially sighted, the Braille Trail. In the Useful Garden you can learn how to use indigenous plants for making tea, dyes, rope and a number of medicines for curing everyday ailments.

On Sunday evenings in summer, there is often a concert on the lawns and many famous singers and bands perform here. People are free to bring a picnic and enjoy the music in the sunshine.

I always enjoy the peninsula tour for its variety and stunning scenery, yet there are many other wonderful places to see.

... What did I learn?

Be a good listener. Watch how other people manage to do what you think you can't, and adopt the best of their techniques into your own style.

Chapter 2
The City Tour

Cape Town is known as the Mother City of South Africa. Since 1601 the area has been known as Table Bay.

The first Europeans to round the Cape were the Portuguese: Bartholomew Diaz in 1488, and Vasco De Gama about ten years later.

It was the 1600s before anyone else landed and stayed at the Cape. The Dutch East India Company, established in 1602, was an amalgamation of export companies working out of Holland. They took advantage of the knowledge gained by the Portuguese and travelled to the lucrative Spice Islands in the Far East.

These early traders found that their crews suffered badly from scurvy and malnutrition — but had also learned that vitamin C countered these illnesses. A ship's medical officer by the name of Jan van Riebeeck visited Table Bay on a return journey. He filed a report with his superiors in the

Dutch East India Company, suggesting that a refreshment station be established at the Cape for the purpose of supplying fresh fruit and vegetables to passing ships. His report was accepted and it was he who eventually captained a small fleet of ships that landed in Table Bay on 6 April, 1652.

My half-day tour of the City usually starts at the foreshore where Jan van Riebeeck is said to have landed. There is a statue of Jan himself and his French-born wife Maria de la Quellerie. I give the group a brief history of South Africa, from where it all started in Cape Town, and then take them around the city, to the museum, to Table Mountain, the colourful Bo-Kaap area, and the Company's Garden.

South Africa's history is fascinating, and I probably know more than I do about the history of my home country. I'm sure I know more about Cape Town than most Capetonians do. This is odd, because although I was always interested in history at school, I was never able to remember dates — and I scored poorly in exams.

Indigenous people

People often ask about the indigenous people who were living in the area when the Europeans arrived. Jan van Riebeeck noted in his diary that, upon his arrival, there were numerous people and too many cattle to count.

These were the Khoikhoi, who were cattle herders. There were also the San people who were hunter-gatherers. The Khoikhoi believed in owning cattle; the more cattle they owned the wealthier they believed they were.

The Dutch immediately started to barter with the Khoikhoi for their cattle, and in time the Khoikhoi's cattle herds became heavily depleted. The Dutch also bought up such large areas of their land that, within twenty years, the Khoikhoi, were so short of cattle and land stocks they became dependent upon the Dutch for their survival.

In 1713, a smallpox epidemic struck and the Khoikhoi people died in their thousands. Nine out of every ten Khoikhoi died at this time. Before long the Khoikhoi, who eventually mixed with the Europeans, died out as a pure race.

The Khoikhoi had some very interesting rituals.

A man could not marry unless he possessed a certain number of animals such as a few milking cows, 10-12 sheep for marriage festivities, and a pack-ox to carry the hut and other possessions of the married couple.

At a Khoikhoi wedding feast, an ox or a few sheep would be slaughtered. The bride was not allowed to eat until the next morning. Her feet would be smeared with the gall of the slaughtered animal and she wore the inflated gall bladder in her hair. The entrails of the animals were draped around the necks of the couple as a symbol of the marriage bond. Their bodies and clothes were smeared with the animals' fat.

The Khoikhoi worshipped the moon as their visible god and regarded an insect, the mantis, as a favourable omen.

Upon death, the corpse was buried in a squatting position. Mourners underwent a purification ritual with cow dung, urine and ashes being rubbed into their bodies.

Like the Khoikhoi, the San people were small in stature, no more than a metre and a half tall on average. The San had heart-shaped faces with almond-shaped eyes, delicate hands and feet, and a yellow complexion.

They had a slightly different experience with the Europeans. The San were hunter-gatherers and relied upon the huge stocks of wildlife, which they believed was theirs, for food. The Europeans arrived and with their big guns quickly reduced the numbers of these animals.

In time, the San people turned to the cattle of the Europeans and the Khoikhoi. The San believed that these animals had no owners, and took them in the same way the Europeans had taken theirs. The Dutch, considering the San to be thieves and marauders, fought back by sending punitive raids against them, where many thousands of San men were killed.

The San people would cover themselves in animal fat as protection, and with their nomadic lifestyle must have looked to the Dutch more like animals than human beings. So they shot them, as if they were animals. Some San people moved north to escape the slaughter, and a few pockets of pure San people can still be found in Botswana and Namibia.

The San rock art paintings are a beautiful legacy of that largely lost people. Without these paintings we would never know what life was like for them. Their art depicts animals and their culture — and the arrival of the Europeans. You can see examples of rock art in the South Africa Museum at the top of the Company's Garden.

Slavery at the Cape

As soon as the Dutch arrived at the Cape they realised they were lacking manpower. They were forbidden by the Dutch East India Company to use the indigenous people, so requests were sent back to Holland, and slaves were imported to help with the manual work. These slaves had come from such places as Malaysia, Madagascar, India and Indonesia. Slaves from the nearby black Africa tended to be sent to the Americas.

These slaves were put to work doing menial tasks — collecting water, looking after horses, cleaning or working on farms. The main reason for having slaves in the early days was to create the vegetable garden for the refreshment station, so many of them became gardeners. Some men were skilled craftsmen while the women often worked in a domestic environment.

The slaves of the Dutch East India Company were housed in the Slave Lodge in Adderley Street.

Sir Charles Adderley was a British parliamentarian who sympathised with the people at the Cape and fought in the Houses of Parliament against the transportation of convicts to South Africa. For months in 1850, a convict ship was anchored outside Table Bay whilst the authorities argued about what to do with it. Adderley was instrumental in convincing the British to find a better location for these unsavoury characters. That is why, when the ship left the city, the grateful city named one of its main streets after him. That ship eventually sailed on to Tasmania.

About 1,000 slaves lived in the Slave Lodge in cramped and inhumane conditions. The building was filthy, the food was dreadful, and with the slit windows to prevent escape, the building let in very little light. Even in the height of summer, when inspectors eventually called they had to carry a lamp to see clearly inside.

The lodge became a house of prostitution, as women, keen to earn a few extra coins, entertained visiting sailors. Many children were born as a result of these activities. The authorities did not object to this behaviour, because the children in turn grew up to be slaves — reducing the burden on the slave traders in far off countries.

Yet, these slaves could sometimes be the lucky ones. Slaves in the rural areas often received worse treatment at the hands of their owners. In town, strict control could be kept on the discipline of slave owners, whereas in the countryside it was difficult to administer and farmers were free to deal with misbehaving slaves as they saw fit.

In 1808 the trading of slaves ceased, and slavery itself was abolished at the Cape in 1834.

The demise of the Dutch East India Company came at the end of the 1700s. The British arrived in 1795, and the second British occupation was in 1806.

The Afrikaners became displeased with the British rule and moved north, beginning the great trek of these Afrikaners (Voortrekkers), in 1834-40, and the setting up of the Orange Free State and Transvaal. Diamonds were discovered in 1867-70, and gold in 1886 which triggered the two Anglo-Boer wars of 1880-81 and 1899-1902.

In 1910 the Union of South Africa came into existence. Soon, restrictive laws were passed and after 1948 when the National Party came into power, apartheid laws were introduced. The African National Party (ANC) grew up to oppose those rules, first by passive means and then, as proposed by Nelson Mandela, less passive methods were used. Faced with international pressure and unrest at home, the government — led by president FW de Klerk — finally abandoned apartheid in 1990. Nelson Mandela was released from prison and the rest of the story is well known.

Table Mountain

Everybody wants to go up Table Mountain to see the spectacular views. For those who haven't been already, an hour is often enough. From the top of the cable car, on a clear day you get lovely views of Robben Island out in Table Bay, and the city bowl with its Victoria and Alfred Waterfront. On a very clear day you can see all the way down the peninsula to Cape Point.

I prefer to walk up the mountain. The shortest route is up Platteklip Gorge, which starts along the road from the lower cable car station and climbs steeply for about two hours. The climb is steep, with large steps in places, and plenty of people pass you on the way up and down this busy footpath.

Another route, provided you have the proper map or a guide, is to start from Kirstenbosch Botanical Gardens from the other side of the mountain. This route takes about four hours and you arrive at Maclear's Beacon, the highest point of Table Mountain, some 1,086 metres above sea level.

To put things into perspective, Table Mountain is two metres higher than Mount Snowdon in the UK, yet it is situated in the city of Cape Town. Many people don't take the mountain seriously because of its proximity to the city, and find themselves ill-prepared for the climb. The weather can be very different at the top, which is three kilometres wide and takes an hour to walk across. A cloud, called the tablecloth, often sits on the mountain.

If the cable car is closed because of bad weather, one alternative is to drive to Bloubergstrand, (meaning 'Blue Mountain Beach') and stop at

Table View for the classic view of Table Mountain, as seen on postcards all over the province. Did you know that Table Mountain is said to be the most photographed object in the world?

Table Mountain is six times older than the Himalayas and five times older than the Rockies, which makes it one of the oldest mountains on Earth.

Composed of sandstone, bedded on granite rock, Table Mountain used to be at sea level. Over many ice ages the upper surface was scraped flat by passing glaciers. Then, 130 million years ago, when the supercontinent, Gondwana, split apart separating Africa from South America, India, Madagascar and Antarctica, pressures built up in the earth's crust. Because of the solid granite base the huge forces were deflected downwards and Table Mountain rose to its present height.

The Khoikhoi called it 'Hoekrikwaggo', 'the mountain of the sea'.

MY INTRODUCTION TO SELF DEVELOPMENT

Can you pinpoint someone you've met, who had a large impact on your life and its direction? I believe it's no coincidence that we meet the people we meet. They come into our lives for a reason.

Once I met a girl on holiday — my one holiday romance. Afterwards, Siggy invited me over to South Africa for a holiday and to meet her family. At first I dithered, but then I decided to go. She became my best friend and has been instrumental in most of the major decisions I have taken since. My life would be very different now if I hadn't met Siggy.

The golf club I belong to has no course of its own. Once a month we have a day out at a local course instead. One day, arriving at the course, I bumped into an old friend whom I hadn't seen for a while. We had what turned out to be a pivotal conversation.

I'd first met Martyn when we both worked for the same company. I didn't know him well and we met in the office only occasionally. I did know he had recently moved to Maidenhead where I was also living at the time.

When Martyn heard I was splitting up with my then girlfriend and moving house, he offered to let me stay with him for a while. I met him at their house to discuss arrangements and it was then that I met his wife, Hilary. She didn't know me at all but was happy to take me in for what was to be two months while my house purchase went through.

At that time they had no children. After I left, three months later, I heard that Hilary was pregnant. Perhaps their rediscovered privacy had made the difference.

I saw less and less of them over the years that followed, as we led very different lives. They didn't travel like me, and I wasn't in the children and babysitting world. Now and then I would meet Martyn to catch up. It seemed to be about every five years, as I heard about baby Ben who was now 6, then 11, then 16 years old.

Each time I spoke to Martyn, he told me how his life was going. On this occasion at the golf course, I left wondering what I was doing with my own life. Here was a man I respected, who had progressed to Director status in a reasonably sized company and was having a lovely family life.

When Martyn asked me what *I* was up to, I was invariably doing the same as when we'd met five years before. I lived in the same house, worked for the same company and was playing golf and squash with the same people. I even had the same car. The only different thing would be my girlfriend.

For days after that meeting I would feel flat. I had been stagnating. Would I ever get somewhere? Where did I want to go, anyway? I had no answer to so many questions.

Suddenly, I saw exactly why I hadn't moved on. It *suited* me to play golf with the people I played with; I didn't *want* to pay the fees for a permanent club and I didn't play that often anyway. It was a similar story with squash. I was comfortable exactly where I was.

This realisation made me feel better and I carried on with my life. But the seed of change had been sown. My mind had opened to something — but I didn't know it at the time.

Later that year, I went on a one-week group holiday to Jordan. Before the tour started, by chance I happened to meet a London-based lady called Annette in the reception area of a Cairo hotel. She was a vibrant, fun and deeply interesting person. Both travelling alone, we agreed to spend the day together in Cairo and visit the museum and Pyramids.

The Landmark experience

Back home from the Jordan trip, I called Annette.

Intriguingly, her phone was engaged for most of the evening. When I finally got through, she explained that she was coaching, adding: 'If you're free tomorrow evening, we have an evening session. You're welcome to come along as a guest and see for yourself.' I was available, so I made my way into London to see what it was all about.

Annette was coaching on a communication course with Landmark Education, a London-based American company that specialises in self development.

Coaching involves supporting a participant, encouraging and inspiring them to achieve their goals from a position of having already done it. It's more about listening and directing, than talking and teaching in the conventional sense.

That first night, I sat in a large room with Annette and many other people listening to an inspiring speaker on stage. Andrea was a lady in her late forties, well dressed in a simple way. She originated from the Netherlands and spoke with the confidence that comes with long training. She seemed comfortable in front of such a large crowd, and she had a way of making us all feel relaxed too.

She invited the audience to come to the microphone at the front and explain a little of their own story. In my experience, at such times people usually hide behind the one in front and the leader has to drag someone to the front. But on this occasion many hands shot up. When selected, people enthusiastically rushed to the front, eager to say their piece. 'Make it short so that everyone can have a say,' she told the waiting participants.

I have never seen so many confident, eager and stimulating people, each with a different and impressive personal story about the changes in their lives. I vowed then that whatever the reason I had come that night, if I could get even half of that confidence from my participation in this work it would be a bonus!

Well, in time I did get that and lots besides — but I had to choose to make it happen.

Landmark Education provides an initial three-part course: the Landmark Forum, a weekend where you put your past firmly in the past; the Advanced Course, a longer weekend where you create a new future for yourself; and the Self Expression and Leadership Programme, a series of evenings and weekends over a three month period, where you learn leadership skills, practise expressing yourself and create a project to help your local community.

Now, I wanted to do the first course — but the date would have to fit around my next trip abroad, the date of which was still uncertain. At the end of the proceedings a man who made all the difference spoke to me. He was just a regular man probably about thirty, but it was his charisma that struck me. I was never to meet him again — but the absolute attention he gave me during that conversation made me feel wanted, even special.

I told him I was there because I'd thought there might be a reason why I'd had so many relationships but had not been able to settle down. Was it something to do with me or had I not met the right person yet?

He told me: 'Half the women in that room are suitable for you.'

That set me reeling. Here was an opportunity to learn, if only I could get my head around it. So I signed up.

Where it all started

It's not easy to spend a whole weekend in a room listening, concentrating and sharing your inner thoughts with strangers.

There are rules about confidentiality and not relating personal facts to the outside world. It's a safe environment where participants can talk freely with like-minded individuals, get support from highly trained non-medical people, and make friends. I still keep in touch with members of that group.

The first advantage I gained was that my ability to listen and concentrate for long periods improved dramatically. I had never been good at this and had often caught my mind wandering. It doesn't any more. It's only practice.

That weekend I learned how common it is for families to have problems, and how many people have been abused in some way or been rejected because of their views or sexual persuasion.

Having heard others' stories that weekend, I was thankful that my own family was intact. My parents were still together. We were a close family but not what I would call *loving*. We never told family members that we loved each other.

So, I phoned my parents and told them I loved them — something I had never done before. I didn't want to wait until I saw them again; something might go wrong in the meantime. I didn't want to lose a parent and regret that I hadn't expressed my love for them. Of course, they assumed that something was wrong. They said: 'Of course we love you, you know that!'

But they had never said so before.

From then on I made a habit of telling my mother and father that I loved them. Many months later, after one telephone conversation, I went to put the phone down and just caught my mother quietly saying: 'I love you.' When I told my sister she was indignant, saying: 'She never tells *me* that!' I now hug my parents when I meet them or leave.

So, I had already affected my family in a small way. There was more to come.

I had always blamed my brother for not keeping in contact with me, and felt his family were wrong for not being grateful for my Christmas and birthday presents. I didn't speak much to them, let alone visit. I was not experiencing his children growing up, and they weren't seeing much of their Uncle Nick.

So, I called my brother. I apologised and suggested we get together. He invited me up to his home. I went twice in the following year, going out for a beer with him and sleeping on the floor overnight. It was a joy to chat with him and to see the children in the morning. It wasn't difficult. It only took a phone call.

Nowadays, I don't judge people against my own standards. Other people do things differently from me. My brother is free to do as he pleases and it is not for me to place him or his family in the wrong. In the end, it was I who suffered for that belief, when I lost contact with them. It's not that they are wrong and I am right. We are simply different.

That there is so much prejudice, racism, hate and war in the world stems from one party claiming that their way is right and everyone else is wrong. If only people could live with the fact that we can all be *different*, there would be less hardship in the world.

That weekend's course taught me that many of the things we make up about ourselves are just stories. Certain events occur and we make them mean something; it is only our own understanding, yet the truth may be very different.

Where it's something we made up, then it can be changed; if it can be changed, we can choose to believe something else. I started to see that we can shape our own lives — a very powerful message. We can have control over ourselves instead of being a victim of circumstances.

Being happy with myself

Over a period of time I became happier with myself. There are still moments when I look at myself in the mirror and dislike what I see — but generally I am relaxed about myself. This gives me an inner peace.

It is this peace that matters most to me. I used to spend too much time thinking about what other people think of me. It affected everything I did. What might the neighbours think? Work colleagues? Everybody, even those who didn't know me?

Not until I stopped doing it did I realise it was going on. Now I have more time to think about more important things because I don't spend time wondering what others think.

Never did I feel totally confident in myself. I always thought I would be found out one day. Outwardly, it probably didn't show. Many people would say to me that I was good at my job — but it would take many, many people to say this before I started believing it myself. I'm sure this lack of confidence has held me back in my professional career.

I was able to quantify the effect of this, after one incident in particular.

To qualify as a Chartered Surveyor, candidates must pass a professional interview. My company persuaded me to become an assessor for the Royal Institution of Chartered Surveyors (RICS) and sit on one of their interview panels.

I became one of two assessors sitting on a panel of three with a chairman, spending a whole day interviewing candidates. It was almost as strenuous and nerve-racking for us assessors as it was for the candidates. That first time I was apprehensive, even though I had been on a training course and had interviewed work colleagues during practice sessions at work. I remember asking the chairman whether I was asking the right questions; he had no doubts that I was.

Then something in me changed.

Six months later, on another panel, I noticed how much more *time* there seemed to be. There was enough time in an interview to listen properly to the answer to my question, keep an eye on my time allocation, and prepare for the next question. None of this had been possible before. I had stopped questioning my ability or whether I was doing it right.

At the end of the session, the other two panellists had sweat marks on their shirts and I had none. I didn't feel exhausted as I had on previous interview days. Worrying had used up so much brain capacity that, when I stopped worrying, I could do a better job *and with less effort.*

That evening I left with lots of energy instead of feeling as if I had been through a wringer.

In my early twenties I used to tell people: 'I wish I could always feel as confident and as self expressed as when I have a pint of beer inside me'. Now, I don't say that. That feeling is there anyway. Something really had changed.

My introduction to contribution

The final part of the initial Landmark programme is to look at self expression and leadership. This involves the participant in choosing a project to run over the three months of the course, to learn leadership skills and self expression in the classroom whilst practising them in the community.

It was 2001 and my uncle had died the night before the course began. That first morning, I kept thinking I should be somewhere else, doing something for my uncle although there was nothing I could have done. Knowing that my uncle's last years had been lonely, I set my mind to considering a project to help elderly people. What could I do to prevent other elderly people from feeling lonely? Unable to come up with any ideas,

I eventually walked into the old people's home in my village and asked them what they wanted.

They said they would like a garden party.

So, I made it happen. It was the wettest Saturday that summer but, fortunately, I had organised a marquee, hired from the local scout group for a small sum. At first, I felt I was imposing on people. However, they were willing to take part. Some of my friends and their families helped, my neighbours helped and even my parents came up for the weekend.

I learned about delegation. I gave a friend the task of organising volunteers to pick up the elderly guests. He was provided with a list of names, some of whom had walking frames, and a number of volunteers with cars where only one frame would go into each car. Delegation didn't come naturally to me, but it would have been a lot to take on myself. In fact, it was satisfying to see it done well without my input.

One neighbour wanted to do more, so I allowed him to take on another task, directing parking at the home. It's more effective to satisfy everyone's needs rather than to try to impose tasks on someone who is unwilling or unfamiliar with what is required. Not being aware of someone's enthusiasm to help doesn't work either.

The course teaches you that doing things yourself brings you limited success. By asking for help, you can achieve much more. This was particularly significant for me as I used to be someone who would keep quiet about a project until it was finished and I could say: 'Look what I've done.' That way, if I failed, nobody would know and I wouldn't be embarrassed. The downside of this is that I don't naturally draw upon help from others.

Often, when you share what you are doing with others, they give you ideas: 'Have you thought of this?' or 'I know a friend who might help you.' Suddenly, your project takes off and is bigger than you'd thought possible. This change has had a profound impact on my successes in future years, which I will talk about later.

The next day, after we had dismantled the marquee, I was driving my neighbours home and they asked me 'What are you going to organise next, Nick?' Their view of me had changed.

Three years later I was to become involved in this Self Expression and Leadership programme again — but this time coaching other participants to create their own community projects. This required me once again to have my own community project. It would have a huge impact on many people and is still ongoing to this day. I talk more about this in chapter six.

Time and time again, I have proved that by telling people what I am doing, people and ideas seem to pour out of nowhere. I've become a magnet for success.

Some philosophers say: 'Ask and the universe will provide.' This is true. Christians and other religious people call this the work of God. Whatever your beliefs, the power is there. But you have to be ready. If you are not congruent — if part of you wants something, but another part of you doesn't — then it won't happen.

Imagine there are angels up above, in a warehouse full of goodies. When you make a request, the warehouse angels prepare to send down your request. But if you then say something contrary to your request, the angels realise that you don't want it after all and put the goodie back.

For years I have said that I want a soulmate and I have gone to great lengths to find one. The warehouse angels hear my plea. 'He wants a soulmate,' they say. Then, just as they are about to deliver, I do something that suggests that I am happy with the way my life is and that I don't want to disrupt it by having somebody else in it. 'Wait, he doesn't really want one. Put the soulmate back.'

I say one thing — but I act in a different way. It has taken me many years to realise this. I am not congruent. When I am congruent I will have my soulmate. So, for the last few years, I have stopped trying to find a soulmate. I have been concentrating on preparing myself for her, as she is probably preparing herself for me, right now!

I have also learned to dream *big*. Having big goals, beyond your expectations, stretches you — and so much can be achieved. With the help of others, anything is possible.

Coaching can be time consuming but it does teach you how to manage your time.

It's normal on the last programme to have five participants to coach. Rather than take coaching calls by phone every night, I try to block out an evening of 30-minute calls, back to back. This means encouraging the participants to ring exactly on time, and telling them that I have another call following so that this call will be effective. I also have to stop the participant rambling so he or she doesn't waste valuable time.

It does work if I am strict with myself and the caller. It's all about discipline.

Off around the world

Confidence was one thing I gained in the early years, coupled with feeling happier with myself. This persuaded me to take a sabbatical from my employment.

I had previously attended an evening run by a company that organises group holidays. The evening's subject was South America and they showed spellbinding slides of an overland trip that can be travelled in segments totalling about twenty five weeks. I was taken with this idea and wondered what it would be like to go on holiday for something like nine weeks at a time instead of the usual two. I had already spent a fortnight in Peru, my first visit to that continent, and it would take many more trips if I was to see South America properly.

At the time I was getting a little stale in my job and was starting to think about the possibility of taking a break. I had already sounded out my director about the idea, and he thought it was do-able. I'd spoken to my friend Siggy who suggested: 'If you want to take nine weeks off, you might as well make it six months and go around the world.'

The seed of another change was sown.

Then I did exactly what most people do — I found reasons not to do it. *I don't want to go on my own. I might meet the right lady if I stay at home.* On the other hand, I had some savings and my uncle had just left me a bequest in his will. I talked it through with Siggy and one by one the obstacles evaporated.

'It would be difficult to find a companion who wanted to go where you want to go,' she said. 'Besides, you might meet a lady on your trip!'

I made up my mind: I would go.

The most difficult thing I found about this trip was not the many different currencies, nor the multiple border changes and finding new places to stay … it was to pick up the phone, speak to my director and ask for the six months' sabbatical!

Doing that would prove to be one of the best decisions I have ever made. I visited 13 new countries and lots of things sprang from the journey — not the least of which was this book.

When I left for that trip, I remember realising that a day does not go by when I don't see the benefit from the self development I'd already experienced. Then, after another month or so, I stopped recognising it: I was so used to the way I am now, I could no longer see the difference. That was an achievement for me. I travelled from country to country not worrying about what people thought about me, and with a greater confidence than ever before.

The journey began in Ecuador before joining an overland trip of Patagonia. I travelled via New York to New Zealand and Australia. I rested in Bali, then flew to the Philippines, Japan and, with a stop over in Seoul, South Korea, before taking the Trans-Siberian Express across Russia and flying home from St Petersburg 26 weeks and 4 days later.

When I returned, I knew I had gained an incredible amount from self development and wanted to do more — so I made plans to take it to the next level.

Taking risks is where the fun is

I signed up for a course in communication which lasted one year. Delegates from various European countries met for a weekend in a different European city at the end of each quarter, which was fun, and by the end of the course I had made a number of good friends.

The course was very intense and we packed a lot into it. With classes, weekends away, coaching calls and projects, my week was filled without even considering my social life, household chores and food shopping. You think you're busy? I'll tell you what busy is!

I learned to shoe horn things into my life and started to achieve a remarkable amount. Sometimes we spend longer thinking about doing something than it would take to do it. Procrastination is the evil getting in our way. Now I just get on with it, and I'm surprised how quickly things can be done. When you miss out the unnecessary things we do, it's remarkable how much spare time we have and how much we can achieve. Now I never say: 'I'm too busy,' because I know that I have taken on more before and I can always do more again.

After the projects I had created on that course, I discovered something that caused me to change direction in my life. I have always been a safe person rather than a risk taker. I used to think before I spoke, mainly so I didn't say something that I'd later regret and embarrass myself. My father had taught me to be careful with money so I would always invest safely. I was 'Mr Safe'!

During an exercise to increase my chances of finding a girlfriend, I accepted a challenge to ask out ten ladies by the end of the week. The idea was to get used to rejection so that I would not be put off asking someone out after the first rejection. I had to get all the negative thoughts out of my head, such as *'she doesn't like me'* or *'I'm too old'*.

I asked a lady out who was waiting at a bus stop and I asked a receptionist at a hotel I was visiting. But then I found that time was running out, and I was struggling, so I rang my buddy (we always have a buddy to support us) and he encouraged me to keep going.

With less than an hour left before my deadline I found myself walking around Sloane Square in London looking for prospective dates! Needless to say I didn't meet my target — but the exercise was worth while.

I found that I really enjoyed doing this. The fun was in taking the risk and trying something new. Not knowing what the outcome would be was exciting. I discovered that taking a risk is where the fun is. There is no fun in playing safe. It wasn't about finding a girlfriend at all, in the end. It was about fully expressing myself, stretching myself and trying something new.

This revelation set me thinking and steered me on a new path for my life. A path that was to lead me to Cape Town.

Back to the City Tour —
the Bo-Kaap

One of my favourite areas of Cape Town is the Bo-Kaap area or 'High Cape', also known as the Malay Quarter. The majority of occupants are Muslim — but not all are from Malaysia. Here, there are many single-storey flat roofed buildings which are distinctively painted in different colours, usually in pastel shades.

The Bo-Kaap came into existence during the time of a French garrison at the Cape between 1791 and 1794, when many tradesmen and artisans came into the area to feed, clothe and provide for the 2,000 or so French soldiers. A sexton at the local church, Jan de Waal, purchased an area of land, built some modest houses and rented them to tradesmen and artisans. These houses later became popular with free burghers or freed slaves, particularly after slavery was abolished in 1834, because naturally they needed housing too.

These houses were generally built with flat roofs and terraced to suit the gradient of the road. They were narrow-fronted, having just a *stoep* or open-sided veranda separating the house from the road.

Here on the *stoep* the family would sit, talk to the neighbours, play with the children and eat meals. Often, at the ends of the *stoep* would be a stone bench and some would have low stone walls. A more practical reason for the *stoep* in the old days was as a protection against dust from fast moving carriages, which would be deposited on the house façade and inevitably turn into mud after rain.

The Bo-Kaap has ten mosques and on Fridays Muslims can be seen rushing to prayer or congregating in front of their mosques.

Afternoon tea in style

In any weather, a visit to the oldest colonial hotel in Cape Town is a must. The Mount Nelson was voted the seventh best hotel in the world in one survey in 2006. Here, every day between 2.30pm and 5.00pm, afternoon tea is served. I took my girlfriend when she came over from the UK. It was something I had wanted to do for years.

We sat on the veranda overlooking the beautiful gardens with the relaxing sound of a pianist playing in the background. On this occasion, the tea consisted of salmon and cucumber finger-sandwiches, fruit and many, many cakes. Every time I went back to the table a new dish had appeared. Copious amounts of tea and coffee were served by pleasant and busy waiting staff. I didn't want to see another cake all week! It was a glorious experience. The Mount Nelson is located just above the Company's Garden.

Gardener's world

The Company's Garden is what remains of the original garden started by Jan van Riebeeck to provide fresh fruit and vegetables for the passing ships.

When van Riebeeck arrived he found water running off Table Mountain — natural spring water that had percolated through the limestone rock strata and emerged lower down as a spring. These waters were channelled into canals towards the foreshore, so that the sailors had less distance to walk to collect water with their buckets. This is why you find street names such as Heerengracht, which means 'gentleman's canal' and Buitengracht, which means 'outer canal'.

Initial attempts to grow vegetables were less successful because of the prevailing winds. Once the direction of the planting was changed to suit the winds, crops grew well. These two factors determine the direction and grid layout of present day Cape Town.

The gardens today contain many indigenous and imported plants from other parts of Africa and from around the world. The oldest tree is a Saffron Pear, probably planted after the time of van Riebeeck's arrival in the 1650s. It is now a little tired and needs artificial support for its ailing limbs — but it still bears fruit each year which is used in local chutney.

There are also an original well and a water pump. It's amusing to see the old oak tree which has grown around the nozzle of a now-redundant pump.

The gardens are a pleasant place to visit, particularly in the afternoons. Their tranquillity is a welcome reprieve from the bustle of the streets outside. Many people sit in the shade, relaxing away from the sun.

Many statues adorn the gardens, including memorials to the soldiers lost in action in the Deville Wood battle of the Somme in the First World War. Also represented is Cecil John Rhodes, who did so much to establish a Commonwealth from the Cape to Cairo.

The gardens are now home to grey squirrels. Originally from North America, they were imported by Cecil John Rhodes in 1900, probably as pets. As has been the case in other parts of Europe, these creatures have devastated the indigenous squirrel population and are now considered a pest.

A number of European birds, such as the European sparrow, starling and chaffinch, were also introduced by Cecil John Rhodes — presumably to make the British feel at home.

In Victorian times there was a menagerie in the gardens, where ladies and gentlemen could safely view examples of the wild animals that roamed the hillside.

The gardens were originally three times larger than they are today. They covered eighteen hectares, where today they are less than six hectares (fifteen acres).

During the second occupation of the Cape by the British, many buildings were erected in the gardens, such as the Parliament buildings, the court buildings, the National Library, the National Gallery and the South African Museum with its planetarium. The gardens remain in this format today. They extend from the main entrance in Wale Street to the museum at the top.

The South African Museum contains an excellent collection of marine life, with examples of the whales that frequent these shores in season, and the large variety of sharks.

Life in the ocean

Marine life in South Africa is popular, with visitors arriving in season just to see the whales. These arrive in June from the Antarctic to calf in the warm, shallow waters of False Bay and particularly the Hermanus area. They can be seen along the whole coastline until they leave in November.

Young whales develop their lungs only in their first three months and cannot survive in the open sea. Once they have matured, the families leave these waters and travel back to the Antarctic. They feed there during the winter months when food is plentiful, and when they travel north to calf they barely feed at all, living off their own blubber. They visit these waters to calf about every three years.

You don't have to drive the two hours from Cape Town all the way to Hermanus to see whales. At the height of the season, they can be easily seen along the Atlantic coast of the peninsula and in False Bay. I have seen a number of whales on tours to Cape Point, much to the delight of my clients who were not expecting the sight. We will stop and watch for a while as the mother plays, rolls and frolics with her baby, in the shallow waters just behind the breaking waves.

Unfortunately, on a scheduled tour we have to stick to a time schedule to fit in many other special visits. We can't stay too long watching whales, or the clients will feel rushed later in the day. This can be a tricky thing for a tour guide to balance.

The most common whale around these coasts is the Southern Right Whale — so called as they were the right whale to hunt, being slow and easy to catch. When they die they float, making it easy to recover the carcass. The Southern Right Whale is distinctive by the callosities around its head, each whale having a unique pattern. The blow hole in the Southern Right is 'V' shaped which gives a unique twin flute of water, 'V' shaped when the whale breathes out through its spout.

Its mouth is huge and contains no teeth — but it does have hundreds of baleen (vertical strips made from the same material as fingernails) through which food is filtered. A whale can weigh between 30 and 60 tonnes.

Other whales seen locally include the Humpbacked and occasionally the Brydes Whale.

Hermanus offers some of the best shore-based whale watching in the world. During the whale season, a whale caller is employed in Hermanus to parade the streets, like a town crier, and call whenever there is a whale in the bay. So you can safely go shopping or eat lunch without missing a sighting!

Surely not dolphins?

Once, I ventured north by bicycle up the western coast as far as Bloubergstrand in the northern suburbs. Stopping for a brief rest before cycling back to Cape Town, on impulse I climbed over the sand dunes to see the view of the beach beyond, enjoy the fresh air and a lovely view of Table Mountain from this unique spot.

I was amazed to see a school of dolphins swimming along the shore just behind the breaking waves. It was as if they had been waiting for me, the timing was so perfect. They seemed to be enjoying themselves, leaping out of the water and crashing out of sight again as they passed me, one after the other. I stood transfixed.

Leaving the area, I made a note of the exact location, not having been there before. It turned out to be called Dolphin Beach! Later, I mentioned it to two friends who lived in the town. Neither had ever seen dolphins there, and one had walked her dog on that beach every day for two years.

Sharks everywhere

On my first trip to Cape Town I booked a trip to go shark cage diving. It was a good time of year and the waters were reasonably calm. We started early with a breakfast meeting before setting off for the high seas.

'I can't guarantee that we'll see any sharks but it's likely,' said the instructor.

The area where these trips run is called Gansbaai (which means 'goose bay'). It is very close to a seal colony, a great attraction for the many sharks in the area including the Great White.

Arriving at the site, we were given a safety demonstration before getting into our wetsuits, and the cage was lowered into the water.

You have to question the sanity of sitting with your legs dangling over the side of a boat whilst a crew member throws 'chump' (bloodied fish bait) into the water to attract sharks. Would I suffer an instant amputation? It wasn't long before the first shark was sighted and we were instructed to slip into the cage.

Seeing these creatures up close is mind-blowing. I could make out the unique markings on each one's nose as well as any damage and deformities in the dorsal fin. It was wonderful to see such an animal so close and in its own environment.

The amazing turtle story

In KwaZulu-Natal you can see Leatherbacked and Loggerhead Turtles. Every evening in the egg laying season (December and January), turtles come ashore to make a nest and lay eggs on the sandy beaches. People plan their holidays around sighting these creatures lumbering up the beach to lay eggs, or to watch the babies hatching and breaking through the sand's surface, before heading for the relative safety of the sea.

For two nights before the terrible tsunami in the Far East in December 2004, not one turtle came ashore. Did they know something?

... **What did I learn?**

Control your own thoughts and you take control of your life.

Accept that people are different and be tolerant of others. Don't try to do it all yourself; ask for help and ideas will pour out of thin air.

When you live your life thinking: ***Anything is possible***, amazing things will happen. Ask and the universe will provide.

And finally ... taking risks is where the fun is!

Chapter 3
The Winelands Tour

The winelands is the only tour I can design myself, to an extent. The tour operator I have worked for has an agreement with a wine estate in Stellenbosch for a wine tasting and a cellar tour, and I am free to choose which wine estates we visit afterwards.

The winelands consists of many new wine regions now — but the principal regions where I take my tours are Stellenbosch, Franschhoek and Paarl. In time, I will get to know the other wine regions too.

My typical full day winelands tour will consist of the pre-arranged wine tasting and cellar tour at Zevenwacht, an orientation of Stellenbosch and a short stop to soak up the peaceful atmosphere. We have lunch in Franschhoek and a second wine tasting, with a final drive through Paarl and a third wine tasting, before heading back to Cape Town.

Clients are well advised to pace themselves and ensure they have a full breakfast before leaving their hotel, as wine tasting starts early and we could easily taste fourteen or more wines during the day.

But the wine tour is not just about tasting wine. It's about the whole experience: the breathtaking scenery, the architecture of the Cape Dutch homesteads, the history of the area and the sumptuous French cuisine.

Grapes are grown in the Western Cape region of South Africa, mainly around Cape Town with its Mediterranean climate, and virtually nowhere else in South Africa. The Mediterranean climate is ideal for growing grapes both for wine making and for the table. A perfect harvest would be attained by an early season of rain followed by long summer days of hot sunshine.

South Africa is the ninth largest producer of wine in the world, producing just over 2 per cent of global output. This is small, relative to the huge producers such as France and Italy, who have nearly 20 per cent of the market each.

Exports amount to about one third of annual production, although many wine producers claim to export 70 per cent of their wine. South Africa's top five export countries are the UK, Netherlands, Sweden, Germany and the US, in that order.

Around ten new wine producers appear in South Africa every month, so there is strong competition in the domestic market. There are over 130 well-known wine producers in Stellenbosch alone, and each time I drive through the valleys there are names of small producers I haven't seen before.

The people of South Africa are not themselves big wine drinkers. Consumption decreases year by year. South Africans prefer beer, such as home-grown 'Castle' lager, 'Black Label' and the Namibian 'Windhoek' lager. Black South Africans generally don't drink wine at all.

Stellenbosch produces a variety of different wines in the region, determined by its many varied micro-climates. Some producers specialise in red or white wine, brandy or 'champagne style' sparkling wine.

What makes a visit to the winelands interesting is that each wine producer aims to stand out from all the others. This variety extends to beautiful historic homesteads, impressive gardens and well tended lawns, wonderful scenic views over valleys and wild animals on show. Some wine estates offer cheese and wine tasting, tasting chocolate and wine, or olive and olive oil tastings. Buildings may be uniquely designed, ultra-modern, tastefully modern or even made to look like a castle.

The winelands is the most difficult tour to learn. Many of my days off have been invested in visiting a small area of the region at a time, on my own or with another guide, to broaden my knowledge of the wine estates.

Stellenbosch

The second oldest settlement after Cape Town, Stellenbosch was established in 1679. The

Cape was expanding and there was a need to find new farming areas to meet the demands of the passing ships and the growing population of the Cape.

Simon van der Stel, the first governor of the Dutch East India Company, rode with a few soldiers out into the countryside. On the second day he came across a river with clear waters surrounded by lush green pastures. He called it the Eerste River, meaning 'first river'. He then found a split in the river and an island, where he and his men camped on the second night. That location was to become the start of the settlement.

Initially, they built a church, a 'drostdy' or courthouse, a mill and some houses. This became the settlement known as van der Stel se Bosch ('van der Stel's bush') and later shortened to 'Stellenbosch'.

For a while Stellenbosch did not grow. The Dutch had founded the town yet it was the Germans who came in numbers, attracted by new opportunities. These German tradesmen had much influence on the town, and many of the roads have German names. Today, about 70 per cent of the population of Stellenbosch speak Afrikaans or German.

Simon van der Stel was a lover of trees, especially the oak. Those he planted in the area give the town its character of oak trees and water furrows for irrigation. The trees provide shade from the intense sun and help to reduce traffic noise.

Their fallen leaves provide a mulch for compost and the wood itself has many uses.

With the development of the wine industry in the area, it was assumed that oak trees would be useful for making oak barrels. Unfortunately, oaks grow quickly in the South African climate and the wood becomes too porous to use as barrels, so these are imported mainly from France and the USA.

Importing barrels is expensive because they are used only three or four times. The oak gives the wine added body: French oak gives spiciness to the wine and American oak a vanilla flavour. After four uses the wood loses its properties, just as a tea bag loses its flavour, and the barrel is sold on to brandy and port makers who don't need such an intense taste. Finally, spent barrels are used as plant pots and bar stools.

When I take clients to Stellenbosch, I usually arrive in Dorp Street, which is the oldest street, where I point out the ancient buildings, many of which are national monuments. There is an excellent Toy and Miniature Museum, which contains many dolls' houses, small yet realistic maintenance garages and workshops, as well as the inevitable train set.

An atmosphere of yesteryear

A favourite of mine, also located in Dorp Street, is Oom Samie se Winkel, which means 'Uncle Samie's shop'. It's named after a former proprietor, Samie Volsteedt, who ran a general store here for nearly 40 years. The quaint shop oozes bygone times. It sells wine (of course), spices, books, hats and clothes, as well as curios for the passing tourist. There is a small restaurant in a courtyard at the back — if you don't mind sharing lunch with the odd domestic turkey.

Die Braak

The common land where citizens of Stellenbosch grazed their cattle in the early years is called Die Braak or 'The Braak'. It comes to life every year, on the nearest weekend to October 14, when Simon van der Stel's birthday is celebrated. There is always a good market on Die Braak, and plenty of interesting buildings.

There were three fires in Stellenbosch's history. The first, in 1710, burned down the original church, the drostdy, a store and 12 houses. In 1732 the first fire appliance was purchased and a number of volunteer fire-fighters retained. Laws were passed to prevent people carrying burning embers in the streets.

The second fire took place in 1803, destroying 42 houses. Oily rags were found in the remains of one of the houses which were traced to a slave called Patientie and a lady called Julia. Slaves often rebelled by working slowly, or breaking their owners' farm machinery, or setting fire to their owners' property. Here, the two accused were sent to Cape Town for trial, found guilty, brought back to Stellenbosch and publicly hanged.

The third fire started in a cobbler's shop in 1875. A pot, containing pitch used to make cobbler's wax, boiled over and set the chimney on fire. Burnt embers flew on to neighbouring roofs and suddenly Stellenbosch was on fire again. They sent a train up from Cape Town with more fire fighters and fire fighting equipment. Then they found they had a shortage of buckets, so a second train chugged its way up from Cape Town — and Stellenbosch was again saved.

After all these fires, many buildings were rebuilt with flat roofs, although some were later restored to the original style. Unfortunately, in the 1950s and 1960s many historic houses were demolished to make way for the more modern shopping centres and the bank buildings of today.

Built in 1777, the Kruithuys or Powder House is the oldest building in Stellenbosch and is one building that did not originally have a thatched roof — for the excellent reason that it contained the town's gunpowder and armoury!

My favourite building, because of its beautiful rose garden, is the Burgher House (burgher means 'free man'). This building is now owned by The Historic Houses of South Africa as its head office. It is a national monument, open to the public during office hours.

The Church of St Mary, on Die Braak, is the Anglican church. Originally it sat only sixty but having been enlarged more than once it now accepts a congregation of up to three hundred in two services on Sundays. The church was consecrated by Cape Town's Anglican Bishop, the Reverend Robert Gray. His wife was a skilled draughtswoman and there are many 'Sophie Gray' designed churches around the country.

Stellenbosch's historic houses

Many South Africans are very religious and in every town the most prominent church is the Dutch Reformed Church, a Protestant church based on Calvinism. Stellenbosch is no exception, and the Moederkerk ('Mother Church') is a majestic white building built in 1863 in the neo-Gothic style, using funds raised by a lottery after the original church was destroyed in the first fire of 1710.

The village museum is a collection of four buildings depicting life in the 1700s, early 1800s, late 1800s and early 1900s. Each of the four — the Schröder House, the Bletterman House (the old police station), the Grosvenor House and Oloff Bergh's House — has its own history and a different architectural style, reflecting the standard of living and affluence of the four households. The houses are equipped with furniture and implements of each era, and a lady dressed in the costume of the day explains life in that house and answers questions.

I particularly like the earliest house, the Schröder House, with its beeswax cloth windows which allow light in and keep everything else out. Beeswax cloth was used before sheet glass was available and affordable to the lower classes. The floors were made of earth with a dung coating which polishes to a good hard surface.

The only other residence I will mention here is d'Ouwe Werf or Old Yard in Church Street. This is now a prestigious guesthouse, each room furnished in antiques. It stands on the plot where the original church was burned down in the 1710 fire.

This area of Stellenbosch contains many cafés, restaurants, boutiques and galleries. It's a lovely area to stroll around and soak up the atmosphere, or in which to relax with your favourite coffee or the South African-grown Rooibos ('red bush') tea.

Stellenbosch is a university town. Until the mid-1990s, if you were English-speaking you went to University of Cape Town (UCT), and if you were Afrikaans-speaking you went to Stellenbosch University. Now Stellenbosch holds courses in both languages.

The Theological Seminary is located on the most historic site in the town, the place where Simon van der Stel found the split in the Eerste River and where the original drostdy was built before being destroyed in the first fire.

In spring, the flowering jacaranda trees lining the roads around the university campus bathe it in a beautiful lilac colour. Driving down the avenues is like floating on a blue carpet.

Resident animals in a land of wine

Sometimes going into the winelands is like going on safari. Vredenheim is a wine estate with wild animals on display at the entrance to the property. Driving past the farm you can see zebra, wildebeest, bontebok, impala, gemsbok and ostriches. Saxenburg also has zebra, impala and springbok, visible as you drive from the entrance towards the manor house.

The most famous animals in the winelands must be the cheetahs at Spier. Nobody expects there to be big cats in such a beautiful part of the country, miles from any game reserve. Spier is an historic 300 year old wine estate. As well as wine tasting being available, the Spier Estate contains a four star hotel, conference centre, golf course, delicatessen, eagle and raptor centre, and a popular African-style open air restaurant called 'Moyo'.

The big cats are part of a cheetah rehabilitation centre and viewing is popular — especially with children. There is a modest entry fee but for a larger sum visitors may stroke a cheetah. The money goes towards the rehabilitation programme. Great care is taken in preparing the visitor and to ensure the animal is docile before visitors are allowed to approach, from one side only.

Handbag Charlie

At Le Bonheur, on the other side of Stellenbosch, there is a crocodile farm housing some 6,000 Nile crocodiles. These crocodiles are bred purely for their meat and skins, and when they reach a metre and a half long they go to the abattoir to be converted into steaks and a pair of shoes. In fact, it takes two crocs to make a pair of shoes.

We met Charlie, the baby croc, and were allowed to hold him. Every day, in order not to stress the animals, they select a small croc and put it in a separate tank where it can be easily removed and handled by visitors. The next day it returns to the main tank and is replaced by another 'Charlie'. We dubbed ours 'Handbag Charlie' as that is what he was likely to become if he ate his greens (chicken actually!).

On this farm, crocodiles are fed three times a week. They are not fed at all during the four months of winter, as their metabolism is too slow to digest food in the colder months.

The short life of a butterfly

Butterfly World is in Klapmuts, north of Stellenbosch.

Butterflies normally live for only ten days, of which they spend eight in metamorphosis (changing into a butterfly). That leaves them two days to live — although they can live up to three weeks in the safe environment of this sanctuary. Butterfly World, like many butterfly show farms, imports hundreds of pupae every week from the Philippines, Costa Rica and China.

Inside, there are other animals such as the funny-looking marmosets with their white fluffy ears and cute little faces. Two of these small monkeys tried to undo a lady's ankle bracelet on one of my tours.

Fairview Estate in Paarl is well known for its cheeses. It has an excellent shop offering cheeses from all over the world. Outside the manor house is a goat shed where the long-bearded white Saanen goats climb an external spiral staircase to enter their home. The goat shed now features on Fairview's wine label.

The arrival of the French

With the arrival of the Dutch, the Europeans started planting vines. As early as February 1659, Jan van Riebeeck recorded in his diary that he had made wine from the first Cape grapes. Later, Simon van der Stel, who also enjoyed wine, planted vines at his estate.

Over in France, where for many years there had been unrest between the Catholics and the Protestants, the (Calvinist Protestant) Huguenots were being persecuted by the Catholics. In 1598 King Henry IV of France issued the Edict of Nantes. The purpose was *'to bracket together all the differences between two religions and expedite lasting peace'*. It was declared permanent and irreversible.

Nevertheless, in 1685 King Louis XIV *revoked* the Edict of Nantes to prevent the Huguenots practising their religion, again threatening them with persecution and death. Many thousands left France and settled in other parts of Europe. Some arrived in Holland but there was little space to accommodate them.

At this time, the Dutch East India Company at the Cape had been looking for more manpower, and especially skilled people, to help with the expanding trade of the passing ships. The Governors persuaded Huguenots to move to the Cape, bringing with them their wine making skills. They were offered land, a sum of money, a free passage and a new life at the Cape. Initially, 200 Huguenots arrived in 1688, with about 270 arriving in total by 1720.

The Company, concerned about the impact that even 200 Huguenots would have on their Dutch culture, gave them land scattered in different areas of one valley. This valley — once called De Olifantshoek ('elephant corner') — became known as Franschhoek ('the French corner').

The new settlers had to satisfy a number of conditions before being accepted. Among these was an oath of allegiance to the Netherlands and loyalty to the Dutch East India Company. They were expected to stay for a minimum of five years and had to pay their own passage back if they left earlier than that. Upon their arrival they were expected to integrate into the Dutch society.

Initially forbidden, eventually they had a church of their own where they could worship in French.

Within two generations these Huguenots were totally integrated into the Dutch society, and subsequent generations lost their French tongue. However, their legacy is that there are many French names in the area; names of wine estates bear the French language; and many surnames remain or only slightly changed — such as Le Clerk changing to De Klerk.

At the far end of Huguenot Street is the Huguenot Memorial, next door to which is a little museum explaining the arrival of the Huguenots. The memorial is set in a beautifully manicured garden and celebrates the 250th anniversary of the arrival of the Huguenot people. The central figure is a Huguenot wife and mother standing on the Globe, carrying a broken chain in one hand and a Bible in the other, signifying freedom from religious persecution. Behind her are arches symbolising the Trinity. The whole memorial is set in waters to mirror calmness, tranquillity and spiritual peace.

One of the delights of visiting Franschhoek today is the many restaurants serving French cuisine. The main street, Huguenot Street, is lined with restaurants and there are boutiques and galleries in the area.

No visitor should miss the Huguenot Chocolate Shop with its Belgian chocolates. The sweet aroma of chocolate envelops you as you step into this small but well-stocked store.

Franschhoek is a beautiful valley with breathtaking views from the surrounding hills. Sadly, fires devastated the hillside in January 2006 leaving the mountains black and bare. Today, the vegetation is recovering well and is starting to look green again.

I do enjoy guiding people around the winelands. It's a beautiful place to be and there is always something new, be it a new restaurant or a wine estate I haven't visited before.

Only a few years ago I was living a less exciting life, commuting daily into London.

TRANSFORMATION

After many years working as a quantity surveyor, I suddenly felt it was time for a change. I had been unhappy with my 'situation' for some time but had no idea what to do about it. So I'd stayed put.

I had always been loyal to employers — perhaps an echo of my father's influence. While colleagues continually moved around to negotiate better conditions, I would only ever have two employers in a career spanning nearly 29 years.

Now that the time had come to move, I simply couldn't see myself working for a smaller contractor or a subcontractor. Working for a large main contractor provided good experience, working on a wide variety of large and prestigious projects.

So, I went from Costain to another large contractor, Bovis Construction, in the slightly different role of management contracting. At the time, I intended to stay for only two years because I felt my future lay in project management. It was the early 1990s by this time, and the industry recession was about to bite — not a good time to change employers. When companies started shedding excess employees I was lucky not to be one of those faced with redundancy. In fact, I stayed with Bovis for more than 16 years. Time flies.

I had been based at a project at Chelsea Bridge and was getting on well there, when one day I was called into the boss's office and told I was needed in Croydon. It's true that they did need me at the Croydon site. The unacceptable part was the two hours of commuting each way, from where I lived in Berkshire. Whether I went by train or by car, it was going to be a difficult journey.

Initially, I declined the opportunity to move to Croydon. There was no benefit in it for me. Then I was informed that I had no choice. For the next two weeks I struggled to find a way to make this new situation work...

One weekend, I was coaching on a Landmark communication course. As usual, I was with a group of inspiring people. Many significant decisions have come from those weekends, and I always get a lot out of coaching, spending time with so many supportive people. On this occasion, we were asked to identify the *real* reason why we were attending the course. In other words, what was I going to get out of choosing to coach that weekend?

Because the commuting issue was uppermost in my mind at that point, I decided I would resolve it by the close of the course on the Thursday night. *That* was what I would get out of participating.

That morning, I was travelling into London with my good friend, Siggy, who was also coaching. We hadn't seen each other for months, so we used the time in the car catching up on news. When I mentioned that I was unhappy about my current situation, she asked me: 'What is it that you really *want* to do?'

I don't know where my reply came from, but I said I wanted to start my own business.

Siggy went on: 'In all the time I've known you, you never go for what you want. You always seem to give up.' That made me think.

During that Sunday morning, I spoke to other people about what I had in mind and at the end of the session we all stated what we were going to get out of the weekend. I announced that on Monday morning I was going to go to work and resign. I had resolved my dilemma! A wave of relief, at having made this decision, washed over me. Although it was daunting, I was excited about my new plans.

Strictly speaking, I didn't *have* any real plans — but the idea was exciting.

I took great pleasure in telling the director who had transferred me of my decision, and that it had been forced upon me by *his* decision to inflict so much commuting on me. Money was not the issue so there was no point in them offering me a pay increase, their inevitable response. I simply would not travel that far each day any more.

It had taken me 22 years to become Chartered (properly qualified) in my profession as a quantity surveyor and I had even said flippantly to friends: 'Now that I'm qualified, I'll probably go and do something else!'

Isn't it strange how we have these thoughts and say them in apparent jest?

I had learned that, in facing a challenge, it is better to focus on the result you want to achieve, rather than on all the obstacles in your path. So, I deliberately avoided talking to well-meaning friends and family who were likely to try to persuade me to stay. 'Why would you want to leave a good job?' I could hear my parents, in particular, saying. From the role plays I had used countless times in my projects with Landmark, I knew how to make this thing work.

Even if things didn't end up the way I wanted, at least now I was moving in a particular direction. I didn't know exactly how it would turn out — but that would become clearer later.

Soon enough, it was time to leave.

My new business

Having left full-time employment, my next obstacle was to get used to having no regular income. At the end of the month I was used to getting a salary, regardless of how well I had worked in that time. This was a mindset change that took many, many months to overcome. Even now, I don't worry so much about having a monthly salary, as long as there is some *regularity* in my income.

I had travelled a lot and felt I had a lot to offer other travellers. So, I decided to start a business offering foreign holidays to people, initially in the UK.

Siggy had been instrumental in my decision to leave my job, and we'd kept in touch. She told me her own job was likely to become redundant, which gave me an idea. I invited her over for dinner, and during dessert I asked her if she would like to go into business with me.

I invited Siggy to be my business partner, not just because I saw her as a trustworthy partner and someone with high standards, but because I also saw her as being able to take the lead if I floundered. Siggy seemed the perfect choice, being a chartered accountant.

With hindsight, that kind of support was not needed. I didn't flounder any more than anyone else might. When working on my own I did have good ideas which moved the business forward. Of course, there are a number of things I would do differently another time.

For example, we rushed into setting up a website, before we had decided how we would sell our product and exactly what the website would be for. As it happens, it was used more to advertise than to sell online. Later, we realised that it would have been better to finalise what we were selling, and then to create a website around it — rather than the other way round. The result was that, later on, when we decided to specialise in South Africa rather than the UK, we had to re-design the whole website, which cost us time and money.

In many ways Siggy and I were complementary, and we worked together well. Siggy was more impulsive than me so it was good for her that I made measured decisions. Sometimes she would kick me and say: 'Make a decision!' if I was procrastinating.

Siggy was a stronger character than me, so I allowed her to make some of the early decisions. I held her in such high esteem that I assumed everything she said was correct. There were times when I thought about questioning her choices but shrank from the inevitable confrontation. Siggy saw me as weak in those circumstances, which I found hurtful.

Later, the dynamics changed. Siggy went back to her previous, full time, career and became more of a sleeping partner in our business. Running things on my own meant making all the day-to-day decisions. There was much to learn from reading the marketing and sales books I had purchased. When it became clear that the decisions I'd been making were the correct ones, I started believing in myself. This in turn boosted my confidence and I began to enjoy the whole business scene.

Eventually, I was strong enough to face up to Siggy when we disagreed. I had changed again! Later, Siggy even complimented me on the good work I had done.

The biggest lesson here was to trust my instincts. Instincts are rarely wrong.

One test was when I decided we needed help with marketing. We knew nothing about promoting ourselves. We looked into paying marketing companies on an hourly basis — and then Siggy came across a South African consultant. He was good at his job, had the right credentials, and had a vested interest in our success, being South African himself.

The down side was that he was expensive and wanted a part of the successful business. This seemed like an enormous risk — but in the end I decided to go ahead despite warnings from well-meaning friends, as he *felt* like the right man and I was sure I could work with him.

It turned out to be the right decision again. Dudley taught me a huge amount about starting and marketing a business.

During one meeting in the early days, Dudley said that one of the ways to get our name out there was to purchase a mailing list and write to people who had expressed an interest in South Africa. After four or five days I was to follow up the letter with a phone call, to see if we could help them in any way. 'You mean, *cold call* these people?' I spluttered, aghast. I resented people cold calling me on my private phone and I didn't want anything to do with this.

Well, I trusted Dudley so I gave it a try. At first I hated doing it — but once I got into a routine I came to enjoy the interaction. I recorded every outcome and began to spot the best times to call and the days that gave the best results. I set aside an hour and a half per session, and would make over 30 calls an hour. Obviously there were many 'no's but I would always move on with the anticipation that the *next* call might be a successful one.

Perhaps I had a particularly disarming manner: I got very few abusive or curt replies. This experience was to become valuable in another area of my life, some years later.

As we were getting many contacts through Siggy and her family and friends from South Africa, we decided to concentrate on holidays to South Africa. This gave our business more focus and was therefore more valuable to our prospective clients — at least, to those that wanted to visit South Africa!

Beating the networking bugbear

I attended business breakfast networking events, and enjoyed them. It seemed that getting on in business was not about just selling your product but supporting other businesses around you.

'You scratch my back and I'll scratch yours' is a sound business principle. It was easy to talk to strangers about my business. I had never enjoyed networking when I was an employee — perhaps because I was not in a position to know enough to carry it off properly — but with my own business it was different. I met many interesting people and there was always someone I could recommend if I met a person with a problem. I was starting to build up a list of contacts and I would travel around to different meetings to see which I preferred and whether there were new opportunities there.

Nearly every week there would be another networking event. I had to practise taking my turn getting up and speaking for one minute about my business. People listened when I talked about holidays, which made a refreshing change from facing multitudes of website designers, telecoms sales people and accountants.

Being new to public speaking, nerves often got the better of me. It was easier if we went around the table and introduced our businesses more informally.

In the end, the business itself became heavy going. Siggy had returned to her old career, and even I had realised this wasn't what I wanted to do either. I was still stuck behind a computer all day, or on a telephone, planning someone else's holiday. Mind you, I did fly to South Africa three times on business trips and I stayed in some lovely guesthouses and game lodges, mostly free of charge.

We agreed to close the business.

During this period I proved that I am creative, something which I previously thought I wasn't. This was to encourage me immensely in the future, as I developed my creative side.

The biggest benefit of this time was my growing self belief. After this experience I could take on anything.

And then, Siggy asked whether I would like to go on an Anthony Robbins weekend with her.

The fire walks

We experienced Anthony Robbins at an event in the Docklands in London, his 'Unleash the Power Within' event, which that year was attended by about 9,000 people.

I had heard about the fire walk he does, and I assumed we would spend the weekend working up to it. Imagine my surprise and horror when Tony Robbins talked about the fire walk on that first Friday evening … that we would be doing *later that night*. But I wasn't ready!

The fire walk consists of taking off your shoes and socks and walking on a long path of very hot burning embers. All 9,000 of us! It was managed very cleverly and only a few people didn't feel able to attempt it when the time came.

We were all told how to prepare ourselves. Later we went outside to see the fire being prepared. As I stood in the crowd, a man came from behind me pushing a barrow full of burning embers, bound for the fire. I could feel the glow from his load as he passed close to me. How was I supposed to walk on that intense heat?

Later, when it was dark, we made our way outside to the concrete piazza and queued up for our turn. Each person was to step on to a mat, where we were viewed by an experienced member of 'the team'. Anyone not ready in their opinion was turned back. It was too dangerous a stunt to make mistakes. When ready, the participant was to step onto the 'coals' and walk the eight or so steps to the other side whilst chanting 'cool moss, cool moss' to distract our minds. At the other end we would step back on to another mat, where our feet would be hosed down to remove any burning embers stuck between our toes. Then we could celebrate our success with our new friends.

I had prepared along with everyone else — yet, as I took my turn and stepped on to the mat, I felt I wasn't ready. I was given the green light so off I went. 'Cool moss, cool moss, cool moss, cool moss!' I shouted, as I quickly made my way to the other side. Soon I felt the cold water on my feet, and was shoved off the mat as another person commenced their epic walk. I had done it!

Strangely, I didn't feel a single burn on my feet. I can understand how we are able to 'disconnect our brain' in some way so we don't feel pain, but to this day I don't understand why my feet didn't burn. If you put a steak on heat it will be grilled — yet my feet were fine!

What I learned from this exercise was that I said I wasn't ready *but I did it anyway*. I can see, now, that I have held myself back in the past by saying 'I am not ready' when I could have gone ahead and done it anyway! The future will be very different!

Another example of not thinking I am ready is my golf. For years I played with a half set of clubs, saying I would buy a new set when I got better. When I did eventually buy a new set of clubs, I said: 'When I get *consistent* I will buy some woods.' Now I have woods, my game has improved noticeably, and I am even more consistent. I found it's easier playing with woods — so why did I wait so long? It wasn't necessary to wait till I was *ready*; I could have moved forward at any time.

The purpose of holding the Anthony Robbins event so early in the weekend is that, after you have walked on fire, you know you can achieve anything.

The second time I took part in a fire walk, at a different event, I learned something else. When I am doing something for the second time, I often find I'm too relaxed and can make a mistake. For some reason, on the second fire walk I forgot to repeat 'cool moss'. Halfway across, my mind was too alert and I questioned why my feet weren't burning. Immediately I felt a sharp sting. At the other end I attended to my foot but could find no permanent damage: I was a little uncomfortable for a while and then it was gone.

What I learned was the importance of keeping focused. When I take my eye off the ball something invariably goes wrong. We can all think of areas in our lives where losing focus loses us direction.

In the spring of 2005, I treated myself to another course. Many business gurus advocate going on training courses regularly to improve their skills. This was training — in life!

The Happy House

I had been recommended a weekend course at 'The Happy House'. It's located in Austria.

It is run by Tony and Nicki Vee, a married couple trained by Tony Robbins himself. The Happy House is in a beautiful setting and a great environment for learning. It's not like going on a course at all, because the learning takes place in their lounge and we are free to relax on couches.

I picked a 'purpose and vision' weekend. The time had come where I needed some direction in my life. Here I was, having started a business, without a relationship in sight, and not having a goal. Where was I going? Why was I on this planet anyway?

When I got there I certainly got what I went for — and a whole lot more.

I had encountered goals before, so this was not new for me. It is said that people who have goals, write them down and view them regularly are far more likely to succeed than those who don't. People who operate in this way are also more likely to be financially better off than those who don't plan goals.

That weekend, I found out what I really wanted and a few interesting points came up.

Whilst brainstorming at the beginning of the course, I realised that *freedom* was important to me: freedom from bills such as a mortgage. Whenever I wanted to do something I always had to consider how I'd pay the mortgage, so I couldn't just disappear for a long time and travel which is what I wanted to do. It took me a whole year but I found a way to pay off the mortgage so I didn't have to worry about that any more. The freedom I felt after that date was amazing.

The other freedom that came to mind was the freedom of open spaces. I didn't want to live in built-up areas forever — after all, I am a country lad! It will take time but my ultimate home will be somewhere in the open spaces. That might be in South Africa or even in the real UK countryside.

In terms of my career, I looked at what I enjoy. I like travelling, meeting people and teaching people things. This sounded like a tour guide, and on a previous trip to South Africa I had in fact looked into what it takes to be a tour guide. Now all I had to do was fly to Cape Town, take a tour guide course, and see what happened. But could I do that?

One day Tony, Nicki and I went for a walk in the local Austrian countryside.

Nicki had previously had an impressive position in the corporate world whilst Tony had a very successful business. Both had given up all this to create a better and more satisfying life for themselves before meeting each other, and now they create meaningful lives for others. They are both very talented and very much in love. They also love their work and lifestyle now.

We climbed up into a valley with a lovely waterfall. It was peaceful and cool there, a wonderful place to escape for a while.

We were talking about the possibility of me travelling to South Africa to start this course, and Nicki asked when I would do it. There was hesitation in my reply; obviously I was unsure about it. We talked about my old job and how I'd enjoyed that. Then Nicki asked: 'Do you want to go to South Africa, or go back to your old job and all that entails?'

Suddenly, I saw the choices I had to make. I didn't like the idea of going back to the same old life. Although I didn't make up my mind there and then, there was a definite shift and I was more prepared to make plans to take that big step and go to Cape Town for three months. Just 24 hours later I had convinced myself to go.

That was the start of a very different lifestyle!

Two other significant things happened that weekend. Firstly, Tony talked about singing lessons and how most people can sing if only they knew how. I tried it and it was true. I sang 'The Power of Love' at the top of my voice and it didn't sound too bad. I have no desire to take singing lessons at the moment, but it was good to know that I could do it.

The second event happened when I was asked to go on stage and tell a story, pretending to be someone I admired. Ever since I first saw Anthony Robbins, I had always been impressed by how he commands a stage and holds everybody's attention. Anthony Robbins is in my view the top self-development guru, who has taken himself from near-destitution to riches in a very short period.

So, I went on stage *as Anthony Robbins* and told my story. I found out in that moment that I am good at telling stories. 'Being' Anthony Robbins made it more comfortable, somehow. I enjoyed it. Tony suggested that I join Toastmasters to hone these skills — something that another friend had already recommended. When a message is repeated, somehow you have to listen. I took this advice later that year.

It was significant to learn that I could do both singing and story telling. Whether I eventually do them or not is unimportant. I now know that I have the ability if I want to. This is better than telling myself that I can't do things, and then feeling inadequate. We spend so much time telling ourselves we are not good at things when we don't really know — we haven't tried. Nowadays, I wonder if there is anything that I *can't* do!

These events have all contributed to boosting my confidence to such a level that nothing fazes me anymore. 'Bring on the next challenge', I say!

Back to the Winelands Tour — Pearl Mountain

It was the Hottentots who thought the three granite rocks overlooking Paarl looked like tortoises, and called them Tortoise Mountain. There were rumours for many years that the mountains contained pearls. These three rocks are the largest granite outcrops in South Africa. The rocks shine and glisten in the sunlight resembling pearls and soon became known as Pearl Mountain, the town being called Paarl, the Dutch word for 'pearl'.

Established in 1687, and one of the oldest towns in South Africa, Paarl developed as late as the 1720s. With a rich supply of granite the town became known for its granite tombstones and prepared building stones. Paarl consists of three long streets, the main street being six kilometres long and lined with its famous oaks.

Paarl became the principal centre for wagon making. The long Main Street became an important centre, with wagons passing from one craftsman to the next in production line fashion. The wagons moved from the carpenter, to the wheelwright, to the blacksmith who fitted the iron tyres, and then on to the upholsterer and finally the painter.

Among the wagons built here were the spider and the buggy, the doctor's gig, the 'Frenchman', the ambulance wagon, the wheat farmer's Koeberger wagon, the heavy Voortrekker wagon and the Travelling Home with its six-foot-wide bedroom, cushioned seated living room, side bags, gun racks, folding chairs, water and meat barrels, and lamps.

When the railway came to Paarl, entire trains carried wagons of all types to Johannesburg and as far as Rhodesia.

One of the more famous companies based in Paarl is the wine giant KWV with its huge factory and warehousing. KWV produces two million cases of wine per year and has a maturation cellar containing 2,000 oak barrels. Their overall capacity is 92 million litres. KWV has the largest brandy distillery in the world, located in Worcester.

Their centrepiece is the Cathedral Cellar with its stained glass windows. It is air-conditioned and contains historic old barrels with beautiful carvings depicting milestones in wine making history.

In another cellar are the largest vats I have ever seen, each containing up to 205,000 litres of port. If you were able to drink a bottle of port every day, it would take you 750 years to empty just one of these vats. KWV held a party in an empty vat to commemorate the arrival of the vats from Portugal and 50 people danced inside. Imagine that!

KWV now owns a number of wine estates in the area, including its model wine estate and one of my favourites, Laborie. I love its beautiful gardens, Cape Dutch-style ancient buildings and the warm hospitality. And of course the lovely wines!

Paarl has a number of historic buildings. The Strooidakkerk ('thatched church') a Dutch Reformed Church built in 1805, is the oldest church still in use in southern Africa.

There are two museums in Paarl. The Oude Pastorie (old parsonage) contains Cape Dutch furniture and brass and copper ware. The Gideon Malherbe House belonged to Gideon Malherbe who was instrumental in starting the Society of True Afrikaners in 1875. He and two other scholars took the adapted Dutch language and produced a dictionary which came to be accepted as the basis of the new Afrikaans language. His house contains the printing press used for their newspaper publications and explains how the Afrikaans language came into existence.

The Taal or Language Monument is located on Pearl Mountain and towers over the valley. It was unveiled in 1975 to commemorate the centenary year of the founding of the Society of True Afrikaners. The monument has three columns which symbolise the Western European languages and cultures, whilst the three domes below represent Africa's indigenous languages and cultures. The artist was inspired by one of South Africa's well-known writers, C J Langenhoven, who described the Afrikaans language as 'a rapidly ascending curve'.

A beauty called Constantia

Another wine region, Constantia, is one of the suburbs of Cape Town. Simon van der Stel was given a plot of land here for being such a successful first governor. He called it Constantia, probably after the daughter of the high-ranking official of the Dutch East India Company who gave him the land. With his love of wine he started growing grapes and eventually Constantia became a very successful wine estate.

After his death in 1712, his estate was broken up following the malpractice of his son who succeeded him as governor at the Cape. The estate became four smaller estates; Groot Constantia, Klein Constantia, Constantia Uitsig and Buitenverwachting, which all still exist today.

With the exception of Groot Constantia, all these wine estates tend to specialise in white wines because of the cooler climate. Their red wines are less full-bodied than the reds of Stellenbosch where the sunshine is more intense.

The wines of Constantia, once highly prized by the Kings and nobility of Europe, disappeared for nearly a century. It was on Klein Constantia that remnants of van der Stel's vines were found, cultivated using modern techniques, and the grapes harvested. Now, the 'Vin de Constance' as it has become known, is available for everyone to enjoy. It is superb. A bottle of the first vintage in

1986 recently sold at auction for 2,000 rand, while their current vintage sells for 250 rand (about £18) per bottle.

Offering something different, the wine estate at Solms Delta, outside Franschhoek, contains an archaeological site. The tasting room is in a museum exhibiting a number of artefacts found during excavation of the foundations for recent buildings. The museum also houses a display showing life as a slave in those hard years before the abolition of slavery in 1834.

Opening a bottle with a sword?

Another wine estate offering something different is Cabrière Estate in Franschhoek. Here, the cellarmaster becomes Maître-Sabreur and demonstrates *sabrage* — the art of opening a bottle of champagne with a sabre — in his now legendary tour and wine tasting on a Saturday morning.

Cabrière specialises in producing the champagne-quality sparkling wines called Méthode Cap Classique in South Africa. Cabrière believes in producing wines designed to taste best with food. The wines have a long 'finish' (aftertaste) to complement the food, where the flavour of other wines might already have faded.

Why can't South Africans call their wine 'champagne'? It's because of the Crayfish Agreement. In the 1930s, South Africa had a surplus of crayfish. The French, who were great consumers of crayfish, offered to take the surplus if South Africa would stop calling its own sparkling wine 'champagne'.

South Africa, like France, uses the 'wines of origin' regional demarcation. Only grapes grown on the estate may be used in an 'estate wine'; if other grapes from outside the estate are used, the winemaker loses the prestigious 'estate' status for that wine.

In South Africa some different wine terms are used. Blanc de Noir is called 'blush' in the USA; a pink-looking white wine. Off-dry, as the terms suggests, is slightly sweeter than dry but not enough to be medium-sweet. Hanepoot (which means 'honey pot' in Afrikaans) is a fortified wine similar to Muscadet.

… What did I learn?

Even if you think you aren't ready, you probably are, so do it anyway.

Keep focused, otherwise things may go wrong. Concentrate on the result you want and you will succeed. Don't bother about the hurdles along the way. Change your focus and you can change your result.

Believe in your instincts; they are almost never wrong.

Chapter 4
The Safari Tour

Not every guide wants to take the one day safari tour because it involves a long day's driving. I get up at 4.30am and collect my first clients around 6.00am. I became one of the select few guides who guided this tour regularly.

Many people don't realise there are game reserves within reach of Cape Town and this trip, in my opinion, is the best.

Our destination is Inverdoorn, which has four of the 'big five' animals, missing only the elephant. It also has cheetahs. It's a long drive, over 200 kilometres each way, which we break with stops en route. The tour is not just a game drive, as there is lovely countryside to see along the route.

The journey takes us in a north-easterly direction, inland towards the Western Cape border. As I drive up the motorway towards Paarl, I give the group a short introduction to the history of South Africa. Then I leave them either to catch up with some sleep or to enjoy the scenery outside. The journey takes us around Paarl and past scenic vineyards to Wellington, famous for its church-inspired education and farm schools. Wellington is the centre for the dried fruit industry in South Africa, and with its links to nearby Paarl, it also produces excellent wine.

Wellington is named after the Duke of Wellington, believe it or not, because no other town in South Africa is named after him. It was going to be named after the Governor, Sir George Napier, but another town was already to be called Napier. Sir George declared: 'Call it Wellington! It's a disgrace that in this colony no town bears that name.'

Father and son partnership

From Wellington, we drive up the spectacular Bain's Kloof Pass over the Limietberg Mountains. A kloof is a gorge/ravine in Afrikaans, so it becomes 'Bain's Gorge Pass' in English. Andrew Geddes Bain was the brilliant road engineer who constructed this road, completed in 1853. The pass, 18 kilometres long and rising to a summit of 595 metres, was constructed using convict labour. It was built with very crude implements, where the rocks were heated by starting fires and then dousing them with water to cause them to crack.

Andrew Bain and his son Thomas engineered many vital roads, rail links, bridges and extensive water conservation projects. Most of the mountain passes in the Western Cape are attributable to the superb abilities of this father and son partnership. There is a memorial to Thomas Bain along the Atlantic road to Hout Bay, crediting him with 23 major mountain passes.

I have to mind my driving at this point, as often I am trying to get to our destination on time and there are many reasons why I leave Cape Town late, so I am usually rushing to make up time.

Having descended Bain's Kloof Pass, we travel along the Breede River Valley and ascend Mitchell's Pass on the main road before arriving at Ceres. Sometimes we see baboons along the pass and once I saw them on the nearby golf course.

The fruit juice region

At Ceres we stop for a breakfast break.

The town of Ceres is named after the Roman goddess of agriculture. Its main produce is deciduous fruit such as apples, pears and peaches. All around Ceres are large refrigerated cold stores.

There is one which, in the early season, has a huge pile of wooden fruit boxes stacked outside, nearly the same volume as the warehouse itself. Over the weeks, as the fruit picking season gets under way, I see that pile getting smaller and smaller until the boxes disappear completely. Then, I see many trucks loaded with these boxes, as they crawl up and down the mountain passes nearby. Many a time I get stuck behind one of them as they engage low gear descending the passes.

Ceres is called 'the Switzerland of Africa' because of the surrounding snow-capped mountains in winter. All the supermarkets stock fruit juices from Ceres, which is sold all over the country.

It's another 45 minutes before we arrive at Inverdoorn, the latter part along untarred roads causing huge dust clouds as we cruise along to our destination. It's not a good idea to be behind another vehicle on this road, because dust is all you can see. However, the area is so remote that the road is nearly always clear.

On the way back I take a different route through the Breede River Valley via Slanghoek. I am always amazed by the beauty of this valley. The vineyards are picturesque, with their patterned layout of vines planted in neat rows. The mountain ranges are spectacularly rugged, with the folding rock strata clearly visible in the afternoon sunshine. We pass tractors loaded with grapes, in season, on their way to be tipped into the receiving bins for de-stalking and crushing at the various wine estates nearby.

After getting back onto the N1 motorway, and if I haven't already stopped somewhere else, I stop off at the trout farm at Du Toitskloof. Apart from a toilet break or an ice cream, or maybe a last-minute shop for presents, the store also sells wine from the Du Toitskloof Estate. There is an opportunity to taste wine before purchasing, which makes eventually drinking the wine you've bought all the more enjoyable.

Shortly afterwards, we pass through the Huguenot Tunnel in the Du Toitskloof Mountains. At 3,913 metres long, it is the longest road tunnel in South Africa. It was opened in 1988 at an initial cost of 202 million rand. The tunnel was built with the help of Swiss engineers using the drill and blast method. Some 500,000 cubic metres of rock was excavated, to be used later in the western approach road, and for aggregate in the tunnel walls and roof. Unlike tunnels in Europe, this tunnel has two bores, the northern bore being incomplete, allowing for future expansion. Should an accident occur inside the tunnel, there are emergency escape routes into the northern bore.

This tunnel saves eleven kilometres on the journey between Cape Town and Worcester, which would otherwise mean having to negotiate the Bain's Kloof Pass or the Du Toitskloof Pass.

On one of my more recent trips to Inverdoorn I had a lucky encounter with a snake. We were approaching the lodge on the dirt track when I thought I saw a snake crossing the road in front of me. It is not uncommon to see snakes on quiet country roads basking in the sun, enjoying the day's heat drawn into the tarmac on a late afternoon, so I know to look out for this. But this was different.

I braked hard, announcing: 'I think I've seen a snake,' and hoping I was not about to be embarrassed by a piece of hose pipe or a rope.

By the time we returned to the spot there was indeed a snake — a big one — and it was sliding along the kerbless verge below us. I slowed to a crawl and we all gazed in amazement at this dangerous creature, so close to us.

At one point it raised its head with its hood opening which confirmed it as a Cape cobra. We found the glass windows between us and the cobra very reassuring, as it slithered over a stone and disappeared into the dry desert beyond.

Armed with grateful appreciation, I continued along our original track. I was feeling rather proud of myself, when — no more than half a kilometre further on — I screamed: 'I think I've seen another snake!' Again, the clients sitting behind me had seen nothing, as I hastily turned around on the narrow road trying to avoid the soft sand verges and stalling the engine in the process.

As we returned along the road there was a 4x4 vehicle speeding towards us. I wasn't sure of the location of my find until the second snake reared up in annoyance at the car in front of us speeding by. When we reached it, the snake again opened its hood to ward us off. It was another Cape cobra, a different shade of brown and a little larger than the first, but definitely a cobra. We had an excellent view of this reptile before it too slipped away into the undergrowth and out of sight.

By now the group were really excited and the bus was buzzing with anticipation. Their safari had already started!

This experience was all the more enjoyable for me as I had never seen a snake on any of my previous day tours — and yet that day I'd spotted two within minutes of each other! It made me feel great for days afterward.

Once we arrive at Inverdoorn, the game drive starts in earnest. Despite being in the middle of the day, when animals are normally sheltering from the midday heat, people see plenty of wildlife. When I joined the game drive on my first visit, I was surprised by just how much we saw — and I was also amazed by how close we got to the animals.

SOUTH AFRICA, HERE I COME

I went home from the Happy House with a clear intention: to go back to South Africa and start a new life. Planning the trip took the whole summer. I told everybody I was going for three months — although deep down I suspected I might stay longer.

During the planning of my trip to South Africa that year I made contact with a charity called God's Golden Acre (GGA). My plan was to visit the charity, based near Durban, and to meet them in preparation for the arrival of the volunteer group I would bring over from the UK some months later. This became the start of a long-standing relationship with the charity, and which I will describe in more detail later.

But this presented a dilemma: where to settle? I had liked Cape Town on my first and only visit. It is where 80 per cent of tourists first make for on their first visit to South Africa, so it's the easiest place to get work. But I also liked KwaZulu-Natal province, the Durban region.

So, should I base myself in Cape Town or Durban?

Before I left the UK I arranged to let out my room at home so as to have an income to supplement me while I was away. I was prepared to use some of my savings too, to get this enterprise off the ground.

I was both apprehensive and excited about my new adventure. In South Africa I only had two contacts; a couple based in Stellenbosch who organised wine tours, and a travel agent in Cape Town. Johan from Stellenbosch had booked two nights' accommodation for me, after which I would be on my own.

In those final days before I left, I was too busy to worry. My research uncovered two tour guide courses and I chose the one that suited my timescale better. I still didn't know where I would be staying and whether I would like tour guiding, yet there was no lack of confidence in my ability this time. I knew things would work out if it was meant to be. Looking back on that time, it's remarkable how well things *did* fall into place.

In October 2005, I flew off to South Africa with a light heart. My career no longer inspired me and taking risks was where the fun was. I could keep in touch with my parents and family by phone and e-mail. If I called them regularly it would make little difference whether I was in South Africa or the UK. The only thing my parents worried about was, what if anything should happen to them; if it did, I would simply fly home.

So, I could leave the UK and I would even miss the UK winter — something I was reminded of by nearly every tourist I met in Cape Town: 'Oh, you follow the sun!' or 'You have one summer here and another back in the UK. Aren't you lucky?' It's nothing to do with *luck*. I *created* this way of life, I *made* it happen.

First, I flew to Durban and stayed at God's Golden Acre, where I stayed for three days before flying on to Cape Town to start the tour guide course. Earlier that year, I remember my course coach saying: 'What would it be like if, when you arrived in South Africa, they knew who you were and you were expected?' At the time, I couldn't believe it would be like that — yet that's exactly what happened. This made it easier to make the trip and to talk with confidence about what I was going to achieve for the charity.

Back in Cape Town

In fact, I was glad to leave Durban because the weather was cool and rainy, even colder than the UK weather I had left behind. Cape Town turned out to be warmer and sunnier.

An airport transfer company drove me to my accommodation. As we approached the city a strange feeling came over me: despite having only visited Cape Town once before, and having spent only four days there, the place felt comfortable, like home. It all seemed very familiar.

I had allowed myself a week to find somewhere to live before the course started. The obvious thing was to sift through the local paper and view the rooms available. I wanted to rent a room in a shared apartment so there would be company. Besides, living on my own would be expensive as high season was beginning.

Then a chain of events occurred that was to set me up entirely. It's strange how one thing leads to another. I rented an expensive apartment for two weeks to give myself enough time to find somewhere more permanent. As a fallback, in case I had a problem finding a suitable place, I enquired at a local back packers' hostel.

A week later I spoke to the hostel owner again. As I was leaving, he asked for my contact details in case something came up. Within an hour he called me: 'Are you interested in sharing an apartment with my business partner?'

The next day the hostel owner took me to see the apartment. It was perfect. When I met his business partner Gavin, he didn't say much but the arrangement suited him too. We agreed I could stay for three months. This had worked out, not through answering an advert, but through people I had come to know. In a word, *contacts*.

The chain of events continued. Some months later, Gavin asked me to guide a group of teenagers staying at the hostel for three days. This was my first private tour.

Then Gavin mentioned a tour operator who had visited his hostel. I contacted them and as a result, I worked for them more than any other company that year. Through getting to know one man who owned a hostel, I had found somewhere to live, obtained my first private tour and come across a local tour operator I would eventually work for.

The tour guide course

On the first day of the tour guide course, I'd imagined myself with a small group of youngsters where I would be one of the oldest members. Instead, I was part of a large group of 36 students, most of them about my age. I didn't feel out of place at all.

The course lasted two weeks and consisted mainly of lectures by Wally, the organiser, and a few specialists. During the second week we went out on excursions, which was fun. Wally was 67 years old then, a Jewish, Afrikaans-speaking South African. He was a chubby, grey bearded man with years of guiding experience behind him. Clearly a character, he knew all the tricks and would stand no nonsense.

The other students were interesting and helpful. Some offered me accommodation suggestions. Although the two weeks I had given myself to find somewhere ran out at the end of that first week on the course, I wasn't worried. Something would come up.

The tour guide group was a mixed bunch: people wanting a change in career, people wanting to use guiding to support their existing career, people who had already bought a minibus and thought guiding might be a good idea, and existing guides adding another province to their existing knowledge of South Africa.

Already I was enjoying the course and I couldn't wait to get out on the road and see some of the places we were studying.

The course included wine tasting and we had to pass an exam in the second week. That was interesting because I enjoy wine and had even taken an evening class in wine at a local college a few years before.

On the last day we were asked to deliver a ten minute presentation as if we were a guide, using one of the tours as a topic. I was apprehensive even though I had some recent experience of public speaking. All 30 of us were to deliver a presentation each, so hearing them all would take a long time.

The first person started at 8.30am, and as Wally the tutor kept the running order to himself nobody knew when they were to perform. This was a little unnerving for everyone, even me, until I suspected that I would be one of the later ones to perform. In fact, I was to be the last but one to get up, and after a while I gave up preparing myself as each speech finished.

After watching all the others, I was called to the front at about quarter past two. Had I not been confident in myself, I would have been a bag of nerves by then. One student was so sick with worry, she didn't even turn up that morning.

In the end, everything went well for me. Just as I was getting into my stride, Wally stopped me. He was satisfied. I'd been enjoying my presentation and would have liked to finish it.

That was the end of the course so most of us celebrated by drinking local champagne at the prestigious Mount Nelson Hotel next door. Then the real work started!

The next six weeks were spent reading and studying for the main exam at the beginning of December. I would study in the morning, and walk into Cape Town in the afternoon to visit a museum or acquaint myself with a new area. I was in and out of the city so often in those days, I quickly became familiar with its layout — more so than many of the locals.

In preparing for my exam, I found I loved reading about the history of South Africa — much of it interwoven with European and especially British history. I also liked the scenery which made it all the more enjoyable. It wasn't like working at all!

Being a foreign student, I did have some disadvantages. I had no background knowledge, unlike people who had grown up there. Everything I knew, I had to learn. And, unlike locals, after passing my exam I had to obtain a work permit before I was allowed to register as a tour guide and practise guiding.

After we had met again to learn our exam results, we all walked together to the tour guide registration office to register as tour guides. Without a work permit, I could not register — not a surprise, yet it was still hard for me. I was stuck in red tape just because I was considered an 'alien'.

It would be fully ten months before I'd return to Cape Town and walk into that office to collect my guiding badge!

Why did I want to be a tour guide? As I've said before, I liked travelling, meeting people and teaching. That sounded like a job description for a tour guide — or a tour *leader*, as I thought of it at the time.

The difference between the two is that the tour *leader* is a non-specialist who looks after the group, while the tour *guide* has specialist knowledge such as the culture of the area. I now know that a good tour guide can do both: managing the group and also explaining his or her specialist subject.

One day I realised that all the elements of a good tour guide are the very areas where I consider myself weak! I feel comfortable talking to individuals and small groups but not to large groups. I consider that I am not good at making quick decisions required to manage a tour group and I am not very good at giving clear instructions to ensure that tourists of other nationalities understand them. All this was to test me, and over time I improved on these apparent weaknesses such that they aren't weaknesses any more.

Maybe I became a tour guide as a subconscious challenge to address these weaknesses.

The 'educationals'

One thing the South Africans are good at is what they call 'educationals' — that is, free trips and accommodation.

While I had my business I stayed in many luxurious guesthouses and game lodges whilst visiting South Africa, mostly free of charge.

Wally explained that it is possible to telephone local tour operators and request an educational. If they have a spare seat they let us go along for the ride to learn from the guide. We just have to pay our entrance fees — although in reality I don't think I ever paid an entrance fee on these occasions.

This was where I learned the most, by watching how the guide performed. Even little things, such as how courteous the guide is and how he or she drives, added to my classroom knowledge. For instance, you can't drive a minibus as you would drive your car, especially crossing junctions where the road camber changes or joining a road from a car park for example, because anything less than extreme care causes your passengers to be thrown around.

My first chance to try it out in practice came in an unexpected way. The tour operator that Gavin had mentioned offered me an educational city tour and I was the first pick-up. The guide, Shaan, was a very likable man in his late thirties. He became interested when I said I was learning to be a tour guide. After we had chatted for a while he said: 'When we have picked up from all the hotels, you can guide up to Table Mountain and I will take over from there.' Either I didn't believe him or I hoped he didn't mean it — either way, the whole thing went over my head.

Sure enough, as we departed the last hotel, Shaan introduced himself and gave everybody an outline of the tour. Then he introduced me as a trainee guide, and said that I was going to guide up to Table Mountain, where he would take over. With that, he took off his headset and handed it to me. I was stunned, as I hadn't prepared anything. I mumbled a few things, Shaan helped me a little, and I got by. The clients seemed to think I did an adequate job.

I was glad to have been thrown in at the deep end — although, had I been offered the same chance a few years before, I would probably have turned it down flat.

On another educational trip to the peninsula I joined a Japanese couple on a boat trip to see the seals. At the end of the day tour the sweet Japanese lady gave me a fifty cent tip. It wasn't much but it was a nice thought — my first tip and I wasn't even a proper guide yet!

A real South African Christmas

Shaan was so friendly, as most South Africans are, that when he found out I was to be on my own for Christmas he invited me over for the day. As it turned out, this impulse was to lead to me getting to know a tour operator.

Well, it was a lovely day. Shaan is a 'Cape Coloured' of Indian descent, a Muslim with a Christian wife. They live with their three children in the Cape Flats area, where non-whites were forcibly moved during the apartheid era. Shaan came all the way into town to pick me up just before lunch. It was a lovely opportunity to be with a Cape Coloured family for Christmas.

Shaan's wife's side of the family is rather large, and with his own Indian background there was a huge extended family. Brothers and sisters kept arriving, one after the other, bringing gifts for the children, and their contribution towards the vast selection of food steadily growing before us. I was given a bottle of wine to open and told to relax, which I can always do.

There were over 20 people there by the evening. I felt very welcomed, relaxed and at home there; the people were friendly and I had lots of people to talk to. It was a very entertaining day, and different from any Christmas I had experienced before.

I had never seen so much food and drink. The lunch table was for the large gathering and we started with grilled shrimps, cold tongue and salad. For main course we helped ourselves to a selection of meats, spicy chicken, broccoli, cauliflower cheese, roast potatoes and wonderful gem squashes filled with a sweet corn mix. Later the desserts appeared, followed by ice cream, and then, later still, savouries all washed down with copious amounts of wine. The men went on to whisky and lemonade but I kept off this concoction, knowing my own limits!

Another family member drove me home around 10.30pm.

It didn't feel like Christmas in the sunshine. In fact, it was very hot and windy and — being an Englishman — I was overdressed and spent the day regretting not wearing shorts as the locals did.

A year later, Shaan again invited me over for Christmas Day. 'Call it an annual event,' he said. So I went and had another lovely day. This time I cycled over and someone gave me a lift home.

My first real employment

On that first Christmas Day, Shaan introduced me to a family friend, Enver, one of the directors of the company he guides for. Enver asked me to call him the following week, and straight away I was invited into his office for a chat. The outcome was that I was to be sent on a few educational trips with a guide, after which I would be evaluated and the company would take it from there.

The very next day I received a call: 'Are you available to guide tomorrow?' Not wishing to seem unready I said yes, but explained the evaluation process they had mentioned. 'Oh, we are short of guides. *Can* you guide tomorrow?' So, I said yes — and I did it!

As you may imagine, I didn't sleep well that night, waking up long before the alarm. I also had to find my way to their office by bus (a 30-minute journey) which was an unfamiliar route.

Considering I was about to guide a peninsula day tour, come the day I was surprisingly calm. As well as learning the company's way of doing things I was also learning how to guide. At the office they advised me just to talk about what I saw in front of me — the best advice I have ever received. It proved not at all difficult to follow.

Having done the trip half a dozen times before with other guides, plus the course, I knew a lot of what to say but I was used to being with no more than six clients. I knew that as a non-PDP holder (the licence to drive fare-paying passengers) I could only be a step-on guide with a driver. This means guiding on larger vehicles — and when I arrived in the office to pick up the client list I found I would be guiding no fewer than 13 people!

Actually, when you are sitting at the front, facing the road and talking, you're not really conscious of how many people are sitting behind you. It was very hot and sticky that day — about 28 degrees centigrade. The hardest thing was controlling the group and getting away from each stopping point on time. Not having slept well the previous night, I was glad to get home to my bed that evening.

By lunchtime, the company had already asked me to guide again the following day — so I gathered I must have done something right!

The second day was much easier. I felt relaxed, and introduced more humour than the day before, when I felt I had been a touch too serious. I had to cope with changing the schedule. Kirstenbosch Botanical Gardens, normally our last stop, was holding an evening concert on the lawns. This meant the traffic would be bad in the afternoon so we needed to visit there earlier to avoid the queues. The change didn't upset me much, surprisingly. As a guide you have to be prepared for changes to the schedule, and it seemed that I was up to it.

For the time being, I guided a few tours whenever the tour operator wanted a step-on guide — but not having the necessary permit to drive for them was holding me back. The situation would stay like this for a few months.

Back to the Safari Tour — top of the food chain

At Inverdoorn, the lions are kept in large pens and visitors get a full explanation of why. I'll come back to that later...

The lion is the biggest of the African carnivores and the only conspicuously social wild cat. It is massive, with a head and body length of up to 3.3 metres, the male being 1.2 metres high at the shoulders and weighing 190 kilograms. The lion is at the top of the food chain with only the spotted hyena to worry about — which can frighten off a lion from its kill if it arrives in sufficient numbers (four to one or more). The females do most of the hunting, being less conspicuous than the maned male.

When I was on holiday in the Kruger National Park in February 2007, we saw the aftermath of a lion kill. Two lionesses and their cubs were feeding from what looked like a wildebeest or buffalo. We could see them clearly but for detail it was better to use binoculars. What attracted us to the spot were the birds in the tree above. I counted 13 white-headed vultures, a hooded vulture and a tawny eagle, all waiting for the lions to leave the area before they could pick the bones. I had never seen so many birds of prey in one area.

To find a lion kill, look out for vultures. The lions themselves will be deep in the grass and are nearly silent as they recover from their exhausting chase, before feasting on their unfortunate prey. It's easy to drive by without noticing, but the vultures give the game away!

A close encounter

My closest encounter with a lion was when I visited a private game reserve — the Mthethomusha Game Reserve — bordering the southern part of the Kruger Park. We stayed at the Bongani Mountain Lodge, in a hilly location and very different to the Kruger Park which we had just left. I wasn't sure that we would see many animals, as the park has very dense foliage and narrow winding tracks, not too many open roads and savannah like the Kruger.

We were on one of three Land Rovers on safari that day when we heard on the radio that lions had been sighted. We were watching a large herd of buffalo when the news came in, so we were slow to react.

When we got near the sighting, the other two vehicles were already there. As we approached slowly, we saw a large flat rock behind which the lions were expected to be. To my surprise, one of the Land Rovers drove up on to the rock. I was sure this would frighten the lions — but obviously the guides knew what they were doing. At that point, I wasn't sure we would get a chance to get closer as things can change quickly in the wild and animals have a habit of disappearing. The man in front of me was getting agitated too and wanted to stand up to see better — and he kept blocking my view with the incessant snapping of his camera.

The guide told us to be patient. We were not to stand up in the vehicle under any circumstances as this would alter the lion's profile of us and he might attack. I was not convinced that my irritating friend would abide by the rules at that stage.

The vehicle on the rock moved away, giving us access, and suddenly the guide drove our Land Rover up on to the stone. The Land Rover engine was so powerful that he did it almost silently, and without any sudden movements.

Now I saw the lions clearly, and was dumb-struck by how close we were from this 'king of the jungle'. There was a family — consisting of a male, a female and two half grown cubs — all lying around the rock in the late afternoon sun. The male was no more than four paces away from the rock. If we'd startled him, with two bounds he could have been in the Land Rover.

We drove away, relieved that nobody in the vehicle had stood up and caused a stir. I have seen lions on very few occasions in the wild, usually in the distance or under a spotlight at night. I will never get closer than that day at Bongani!

Canned hunting

The lions at Inverdoorn are housed in cages because they are refugees from breeding farms where they are bred to be shot by anyone willing to pay the huge sums demanded (in the order of 300,000 rand) just to be able to say they have shot a lion. In reality, these lions have never been in the true wild and the paying hunter only has to point his gun into the cage and fire. He then takes home the skin of the lion as a trophy and claims to have shot it — which is true, he did. This *sport*, if you can call it that, is dubbed 'canned hunting'.

The Government and conservationists are trying to stamp out this trade — but with many farms secretly involved, it is difficult.

If it is not shot in the cage itself, the only moment of freedom this animal experiences is if it is let out into the open before being faced with the inevitable. It is a frightening time, finding itself in the open, having been in a cage all its life. Its life is short now as it is attacked by hunting dogs and then the paying hunter arrives with his gun.

A lion park in the Winelands?

The Drakenstein Lion Park, near Paarl in the Winelands, is a park set up solely to look after unwanted lions saved or discarded from public parks. It opened in 1999 and is a privately funded facility providing lions in distress with sanctuary, where they are safe from abuse and persecution, and treated with the compassion and respect they deserve. All the animals brought to the Park are captive bred or hand reared and cannot be rehabilitated to the wild.

We timed our first visit to coincide with feeding time. There were fourteen mature lions and lionesses in large compounds of this 6,000 square metre park. The lions are fed three times per week.

Each lion was given four or five chickens each. They take only minutes to devour a chicken, complete with the feathers which aid their digestion. These lions looked healthy enough, but I was totally unaware of their past and their almost certain future had they not been rescued. The park is having to expand and provide more space to cater for more incoming lions.

As we returned to the reception area for a cool drink, after being out in the burning heat, I turned to see the yellow-billed kites arrive, looking for titbits left by the big cats. It seems they know what time feeding is. The temperature was approaching

30 degrees and it was hard to stay out in the heat for too long.

... What did I learn?

It's the people I have come to know that have opened doors for me.

Many times I have been thrown in at the deep end, and I always accept the challenge. The situation feels uncomfortable at first but I always swim.

Sometimes others see a capability in me that I can't see in myself. It moves me forward and I am glad of the opportunity.

Table Mountain

African Penguin

Camps Bay, Cape Town

Vergelegen Wine Estate

A typical house we build for GGA

The food drop

Kynsna lourie

Lilac-breated roller

Chapter 5
The Township Tour

There is a very good museum in Cape Town called the District Six Museum. It is located in an old church building, on the western outskirts of the city opposite the police station.

It has an interesting book shop, inexpensive compared with the High Street shops. Visiting the small tea room before it's too late in the morning, I can have a nice cake with my tea or coffee. It's a peaceful place to chill out in the company of a friendly face or two. I often have a question to ask Noor or Joe, the two men who manage the museum.

The museum was founded in December 1994 to celebrate the lives of residents who lived in the area before the forced removals took place. Its walls are lined with the stories of residents. One thing that stands out in these stories is how they all lived in harmony despite coming from many different races, backgrounds and religions. There seemed to be a firm level of discipline there, whereby anyone who stepped out of line was dealt with by the 'seniors' of the community. There was a respect amongst the people and racism was not tolerated.

Most of the residents were mixed race working class people. They were very religious — as were many people in those days — and all regularly visited their local churches and mosques.

During the apartheid era the government of the time enacted the Group Areas Act which designated District Six (the sixth municipal district of Cape Town) as a 'whites only' area. Anyone who was 'non-white' was required to leave. In 1966 the government bulldozers arrived and started to demolish the buildings. It took 16 years for the whole area to be cleared. Imagine what it must have been like to live in that vicinity, knowing that the bulldozers were coming ever closer and might one day reach *your* house.

Eventually, everybody was forcibly moved out of the area and given accommodation in what came to be called the 'Cape Flats', located miles away from the city around the back of Table Mountain. Before the move, workers had only to walk into the city to work — now they were forced to take a taxi or train which increased their weekly spending.

Families were given homes by the government which were simple in structure and smaller than their old homes. They lost their former neighbours and friends and found themselves living next door to strangers. The main reason the forced removals were slow is that it was dictated by the speed at which the government could build new houses.

Noor tells us that he was one of the lucky ones: his family was able to move into another family home away from the Cape Flats.

The government demolished everything except the churches and mosques, fearing a backlash from the Church.

Residents returned to District Six every week to worship in their original churches, as they still do today. They needed something to hang on to and it made the transition more bearable if they could maintain contact through their churches.

District Six today

It is a strange sight. Since the 1980s nobody has built on the land. It was hoped that modern developers would arrive and erect new houses and commercial developments in the area but most developers sympathised with the residents and felt the government had gone too far. Also there was uncertainty whether the residents might later prove their land rights and be able to return to their former homes. Nobody wants to own a building on disputed ground.

Today, there are a few residential buildings in the corner of the plot, the only building constructed in those early days being the Cape Technicon University.

District Six was one of 40 areas designated white-only. When I first spent time in Simon's

Town I visited the Simon's Town Museum where there was a display of the life and times of the people forcibly moved from that area to Ocean View many miles away.

There were no shops, medical facilities, churches or entertainment. The government-built houses were small and poorly constructed. Furniture would not fit and had to be sold cheaply or given away — there was so much of it being sold. Kitchens were small and bathrooms had no room for a bath. The strong wind blew sand in everywhere.

The men had to get taxis back to Simon's Town for work each day.

Now, Ocean View has all the modern facilities and everyone seems happy. It's the same with the residents of District Six yet the claims for land rights continue.

Some of the older residents believed they were too old to change. Many of them died of depression and a broken heart. Fearing the trauma of moving, some committed suicide. A few people remain bitter about what the government did and are unable to move on emotionally. I met one such man in Simon's Town who became very angry when I even mentioned the subject. His wife had moved on but he would still get upset even though the government had completely changed.

On a city tour one day, I stopped in District Six while we discussed the events of the past. A battered old pale blue VW Beetle drove past slowly and parked a little in front of us. The driver had seen the tour bus and now came over to speak to us.

With tears in his eyes, he told us he had once been a resident here and often drove through the district to reminisce after dropping off his brother in town. He was bitter about what had happened to him and his family and was unable to forgive those responsible. It was a very emotional moment for us all.

In the days of apartheid there was a hierarchy amongst the three racial classifications: whites were first, coloureds were second and blacks were last. This hierarchal system is still in place today — in reverse. One coloured person told me recently that today the blacks have the upper hand and are first in line for jobs and other privileges. Before the present government, whites had the first choice and the blacks were last, but the coloureds were always second and still are to this day. Their status has not improved under the new government rules.

Restrictions of the suppressed

Many new rules were introduced by the apartheid government to suppress the non-white communities. One such law made it an offence to mix whites with non-whites. As we sat in that tour bus I showed the group the church opposite with two front doors: one for whites and one for non-whites. Bridges had a barrier down the middle, for whites to walk one side and non-whites the other. Even ambulances were 'designated' which meant that if a black man was seriously injured and a 'whites-only' ambulance was the only one in the area, the man could not be treated and was likely to die. Park benches displayed signs saying 'whites only'.

The Pass Laws meant that every black South African over the age of sixteen had to obtain a pass book containing permission to move around the surrounding areas. They spent hours queuing to get permission to move — and these passes had to be renewed every two weeks which meant more queuing. Often they would be told it was too late before they reached the front, and had to come back again in the morning. Queuing became a way of life.

Everybody was required to have an identity card and each race was designated differently. If you were stopped in the street without your identity card, stiff penalties were imposed and arrest was imminent. Identity cards are still in place today but there is now a law *against* defining somebody's racial status on it.

The government introduced tests to identify the race of individuals, as there were so many mixed couples that the colour of someone's skin was not always enough.

As black people tended to have curly hair, the pencil test came into existence. If the hair could retain a pencil the person was designated *black*. If the pencil fell out or their skin was non-white he or she was designated *coloured*. Black people tried various ruses to improve their status. One such trick was to shave off their hair so that it could not retain a pencil.

The authorities then came up with the pin test. When the individual was not expecting it, the government officer would prick the person with a pin. If the person screamed 'Alcka!', a black South African word, they were designated *black* and if they screamed something else like 'Ouch!', they were designated *coloured*.

A small township

I don't often visit the townships. I leave it to the local guides to guide there because they know the area well and can gauge the mood of the people — who can be volatile, especially after being paid at the end of the week. It also provides a local person with a job which I don't want to take away from them.

A township is a formal or informal settlement of generally black people outside many cities in South Africa. The four main townships around Cape Town are Khayelitsha (the biggest), Langa, Nyanga and Gugulethu. These townships are home to over two million people.

The first sight a tourist has of Cape Town after leaving the airport is the adjacent township of Langa.

It's a shame that the most visible part of a township is the informal houses around the perimeter, commonly called shacks. Whilst the government is working hard to build new houses for everyone in the interior of the settlement, there is always someone new arriving and building a house on the outside. These shacks are clearly visible to passers by from the road and give the impression that the government is not doing anything to resolve the housing problem.

In reality, the government is working hard — but it is a mammoth task. The government has promised a home to everyone in the country, and to anyone coming into the country. In the elections in March 2006, I remember politicians promising everybody a home by 2010, which has now been extended to 2014. Based upon current performance the government will fall short of their target but I wish them luck.

Non-government organisations and private individuals also help to provide homes for these people. A well known group of Irish bricklayers travel to Cape Town each year and builds a large number of houses in the township of Imizamo Yethu, just outside Hout Bay, which is along the Atlantic coast from the city. In a short time they built 116 houses during their visit in 2006. Apparently, this township was allocated for 480 families; it has now grown to more than 19,000 occupants.

When I visited Imizamo Yethu I was guided around by a local guide. I couldn't get hold of the guide from the telephone number on his brochure so I decided, as I was in the area, to wait for the hop-on hop-off bus from where I knew he obtained business. Sure enough he was there.

I was surprised to find that some Europeans choose to live here, perhaps because it's so cheap. This isn't at all like the large townships such as Langa, where the houses have electricity and water is available, if only from a standpipe in the street. There is 40 per cent unemployment in the township and 40 per cent of occupants have AIDS. There is a clinic in the settlement as well as a craft shop.

Some of the houses here are very nice and one is particularly elegant, owned by the Senior of the township. People who become wealthy in comparison to the rest still choose to stay in the community so they can maintain contact with the community and engage in celebrations and other activities of their culture. It is different in the west where we tend to move up to a 'better area' when the opportunity arises.

I was surprised to see that this expensive home had burglar bars on the windows and doors. It seems that when you go up in the world and have a better property you still have to protect yourself against those that don't have such luxuries, even in a township like this.

Much of what I saw was very similar to what I had seen at other townships elsewhere, but here one interesting fact stuck in my mind: the guide said that some homes have their own bathroom facilities, but some have to share a toilet block. I can't believe this is accurate, but he told me that seven hundred people share a block of four toilets. Over 24 hours these toilets must be in constant use.

An uneasy visit

My first visit to a township was to Langa during our tour guide course. It was a strange experience and one which I am not entirely happy about.

We all piled off the coach, with over thirty of us milling around a market area watching the day to day goings-on around us. What I shall never forget was the meat on open display. There were butchers in a nearby street, it's true, but there were also open stalls where meat and offal were being carved up. It was impossible to identify what the meat was, mostly skin, fat and entrails.

Travelling around the township in such a large group made me feel uncomfortable. Locals were looking at us as we looked at them. It was obvious why we were there. I felt better when we stopped in a bar called a 'shebeen' where I bought a drink. At least I felt I had contributed something. Others felt the same, as I found out afterwards.

I was in two minds about township tours then. They are a good thing if the visitor contributes to the local people in some way. But if a tour operator just takes people into the area for a look and then leaves, and all the tour revenue goes into his own pocket, then tours are a bad idea.

On this township tour in Langa we visited a local guesthouse called Vicky's B&B where you can stay for the equivalent of less than £15 per night — but there's no bathroom. I have to say this was not the best tour I had been on! I have since had better experiences.

TOWNSHIPS, TOURS AND PUTTING DOWN ROOTS

Some months later I acquired my first private tour. I was asked by Gavin (from whom I was renting a room) to guide a group of 19 eighteen year old students and their teachers from a school in Norway. I was to guide them for three days and one trip on the last day was to be a township tour. They wanted to visit Langa to see the local community day centre.

When Gavin asked me if I could guide the group in the township, I said: 'Yes, I'll do it,' even though I had only been there once before and didn't know a local guide whom I could use.

It's not safe to enter a township without a local guide who knows the area well, but I wasn't going to turn down the opportunity of work. I would find a way!

When the time came to think about the township tour, I rang someone I knew from the course about a social meeting, and happened to ask him if he knew of a local township guide. He gave me the number of a local man called Khanyiso.

Khanyiso asked me questions about my requirements. It was apparent that I needed to see the area before I could understand what was available for us and to even talk to the group about the tour. So, I arranged to meet Khanyiso for an introductory tour that afternoon. We would meet at the District Six Museum, where all good township tours start. When I eventually met Khanyiso, he took me for a tourist. Dressed in shorts and a T-shirt, I probably wasn't dressed like a tour guide.

As I didn't have a car in those days we had to travel by minibus taxi. Khanyiso often reminds me how we turned up that day in the township in a taxi, where normally tourists arrive in a tour bus or private car.

Within 24 hours I had gone from not having a clue how to do the tour to finding a guide and having an introductory tour. Now I knew enough about the township and I felt ready.

Khanyiso's tour

This was a very interesting and educational tour for me. Khanyiso was born and bred in the township and knew it well. First, he took me to the craft centre where visitors have an opportunity to buy locally produced products. I was particularly surprised and amused by a pair of shoes made from an old tyre. The tread of the tyre was the sole of the shoe. The shoes were well made and because of the solid rubber tyre they were very heavy. It was funny to see a Michelin or Firestone tyre pattern on the sole of the shoes. I am sure they would last someone a lifetime providing they don't get a puncture!

The shebeen was a place I would feel uncomfortable about entering without a local guide, especially when there is a potential to meet intoxicated people. I didn't have to worry as it was very civilised. I was almost tempted to pick up a snooker cue and give someone a game.

One place I was keen to visit was the local doctor. Here I met the local medicine man — however, it was only when the group arrived on the next visit that I understood how it all worked. It was like entering a large tent with a low ceiling. Hanging from every available fixing was an array of dried herbs, fish bones and other familiar and unfamiliar objects. His solution to every ailment was to be one of his potions, something I found very unappetising after he had explained the contents.

Men are drawn to the cities by the promise of work. Initially they leave their families behind in the countryside; in this case those living around Cape Town mainly come from the Eastern Cape Province. They sleep in rooms which have many beds. One man will sleep in the bed at night and another man will sleep in the same bed during the day whilst the other is working. The tiny rent they pay for the room enables them to send money home to their family whom they probably see only once a year.

In a slightly larger block we saw a room where fifteen people from three families lived. There was a kitchen area and a lounge but very little privacy.

Many of the residents of these townships work in the tourist industry. They often have to travel long distances. One girl I was speaking to recently was serving in a shop at Cape Point. She said she finishes work at 6pm and is then bussed home which takes two hours. She will be back again in the morning — a four-hour journey just to get to and from work.

One January, just after New Year, I travelled by coach to visit Siggy who was in East London visiting her family, a 17-hour drive along to the Eastern Cape. I found myself among a large group of local people travelling back to visit their families for the Christmas holidays.

I had booked a ticket on a coach operating between Cape Town and either Durban or Johannesburg. The journey, whilst long, was considerably cheaper than an airline flight.

On the trip home from the township, the Norwegian teacher of the group I had guided told me he came over each year with a different group of teenagers. The tour is primarily to educate the youngsters studying a particular subject about Africa and teach them more about the way of life. They always visit a township, so that students can appreciate their own lifestyle when faced with the relative lack of opportunities given to poor people in these areas. The teacher wanted to visit the day centre to enable the teenagers to contribute something.

Khanyiso said the centre was off-limits now, unless a more formal approach was made — which takes time. So, we made alternative arrangements in Langa and the students still got their insight and were able to contribute.

We visited a pre-school and many of the girls fell in love with the children. They all sang songs to each other. The children started singing with encouragement from their teacher, and the display included individual dancing. Then it was the turn of the students who sang a song about their 'eyes, nose and mouth' in Norwegian. Even I had a lesson in Norwegian as I joined in. It was great fun and the local children watching clearly enjoyed it!

As we left the little schoolhouse, the children ran to the perimeter fence to wave goodbye. They obviously didn't want us to leave. Some of the students wanted to take a child home with them. It was a very emotional moment and they told me afterwards it was one of the highlights of their whole tour.

On the way back to Cape Town, the leader of the group commented that I had a lot of knowledge despite not having been in the city for that long. It was a nice compliment seeing I had done only a few guided tours by then. He said my tour was better than last year's, and that he had been doing this trip with students for eleven years. So again, I felt I must be doing something right!

The trip to Langa with the students was a great success. Not financially for me, as I had to pay the local guide out of my own fee, but I didn't mind — Khanyiso was excellent and it was very worthwhile.

When I initially met this Norwegian group for their first tour they told me they had arrived from Norway with -20 degree temperatures, to +25 in South Africa — quite a temperature leap! I encouraged them to drink lots of water to combat the temperature difference and they responded by asking to stop for toilets all the time. Just like children they always wanted to go 'NOW!' On one occasion I had to ask the driver to pull over and just about the whole group left the bus, milling amongst the bushes, with the girls instructed to go one way and the boys the other.

Putting down roots in Cape Town

To drive and guide in South Africa, I needed a Public Driving Permit (PDP). Soon after sorting out my accommodation on my first return to Cape Town, I went into the Traffic Department, an arm of the police which deals with these matters, and enquired about a PDP. I naïvely assumed that I could just go in, flash my UK driving licence and be given a permit.

First I was asked for an identity number. When I said I didn't have one I was told the only way to get a PDP was to take the driving test. Well, I had been driving for nearly thirty years, why would I have to prove myself to them? I was also slightly afraid that I might have a few bad driving habits and wouldn't pass such a test now.

After much deliberation, I asked how long it would take. 'It will take six months for the learner's test (the written exam) and another six months for the driving test,' came the reply. How ridiculous! I was only going to be in the country for another two months at that time. But it takes that long because of the backlog of applicants.

A year or so previously, this might have been easier but not now as the authorities have been tightening up. In previous years they had given out PDPs like confetti, resulting in too many minibus taxis on the road. These minibus taxis provide a stopping service from the suburbs to the city all over South Africa, and for a small fare are more regular and flexible than the public buses. Whilst these minibus taxis provide a service to mainly black South Africans, the drivers rarely obey traffic laws and have no regard for other road users. Many of the vehicles are unroadworthy. The government is now offering financial incentives for the owners to renew their vehicle or leave the business altogether.

A friend advised me not to use these taxis, even before I arrived in South Africa, and I rarely do.

Minibus taxis stop anywhere along the street, usually just in front of other drivers, blocking roads and piling people in until the vehicle is crammed. The drivers are not very good and they blow their horn to attract business everywhere they go, which is illegal as well as annoying. The police do little about it, and when they do have a purge the minibus taxi drivers complain about being victimised.

The first time I ever used a minibus taxi, the sliding door had jammed. The driver had to leave his seat, take a tyre lever around to the side of the minibus and gemmy the door back onto its runners before letting the passengers out. Even his colleague collecting the money inside was powerless. The driver had to repeat the exercise to allow me to depart at the next stop.

Another minibus taxi I used stank of neat petrol. I could only get a seat in the very back and the smell was so strong it made me feel sick.

Nowadays if I need to use one, I am very selective. It's difficult to flag down an approaching minibus taxi, waiting until it is close enough to see whether it is roadworthy. Sometimes I change my mind and let it go if it looks tatty.

Registered taxis with meters are available in South Africa. They are relatively expensive compared with South Africa's generally cheaper prices.

It was at this time that I decided to extend my stay in South Africa to six months. I needed this time to get my licence. More importantly, I wanted to make sure that guiding was what I wanted to do. I couldn't go home feeling uncertain about whether I liked my new career, so I needed more experience. It was straightforward enough, apart from more queuing, to apply for a three month extension to my holiday visa and pay the additional fee.

After my bad news at the Traffic Department, and to get a better date for my test, I tried many of the other local testing centres in the area. I could get a sooner date — but then I would have to find my way there each time. And I didn't have transport.

As I happened to be living opposite the Traffic Department in Cape Town, it was logical to pursue my PDP at that office. I could just cross the road and ask for a cancellation. So I did. I bought a manual about the learner's test and studied it. When I felt ready I went into the Traffic Department and asked about a cancellation.

The Traffic Department is a grim place. Apparently the authorities sacked many of the employees and didn't replace them, creating a backlog. The downstairs is made up of a series of counters with queues of people snaking from each window. When an assistant raises his or her window blind in the morning they are faced with a long queue of frustrated and tired people. It must be a very depressing sight.

To ask for a cancellation I had to see the inspector. This meant queuing outside his office. When the inspector saw the date I had been given he barked at me: 'Come back in at least two months. There are thousands in front of you!' Extenuating circumstances cut no ice with him.

Clearly, this man wasn't going to help me. But there was sometimes a different inspector on duty, so I waited until another day and repeated the exercise.

This inspector was more sympathetic and asked me to come back another time. I had already learned in South Africa that, if you don't get the answer you want, try someone else.

Within a few days of popping in and out of the Traffic Department, I was squeezed in. I was going to take the test!

We were led to a prefabricated outbuilding, set out like a classroom, where the rules of the test were read out. The multiple choice questions were not easy — and some were actively misleading, and aimed at tricking candidates. Many of the younger students finished much sooner than me. After time was up the papers were collected and marked in front of us. We all sat patiently. One by one, the successful candidates were called to the front, and told to sign a form and collect their updated learner's licence.

In this test, you have to pass in all three categories: general driving, signs and controls. When my turn came I was two points short on my signs. After all that coaxing and persuasion, I had failed! I could have kicked myself. Immediately, I applied for a new date and went home to consider my position.

A friend suggested I go back the following day and take it again, but I knew from experience that if I had failed it, there must be a reason. So, I spent the next few days studying my signs. A week later I got another chance, re-sat the test and passed. I was jubilant! But I still had another hurdle — the driving test itself.

After all this time I was getting to know the Traffic Department. I had spent many hours waiting at counters or sitting in the waiting room, hoping to see the inspector. I began to recognise the traffic cops who occasionally passed through the building with their belts loaded with armaments, tear gas guns and batons. I became friendly with the man at the driving test counter and others became familiar with me too. It felt like being part of a family. I saw the anguish of youngsters who had failed their test and thought there was no alternative but to wait six months for a re-test. I now knew the best times to go into the building when it would be quieter with fewer queues. I was becoming an expert.

Finding George

Driving instructors advertise by putting their telephone numbers on their heavy goods vehicles. So, I rang around to find one. I wanted a lesson or two before the test to check for any bad habits, and because I needed to know about the vehicle pre-inspection check which I'd heard was part of the test. My instructor, George, was an ex-examiner. He told me to disregard the manual in places — he knew what they would test on. He was right.

After two lessons, George suggested I get an early test date so we could schedule a final lesson beforehand. So I went in to seek a cancellation. This time I met the unhelpful inspector who again told me what I didn't want to hear: 'Come back in a few months!' George suggested I speak to the more friendly inspector.

Sitting outside his office upstairs, I waited patiently for the inspector's attention and then explained my predicament. I wasn't confident I had a valid enough reason to be treated differently to anyone else — but I asked anyway. He advised me to wait downstairs as he would be down in a minute and it would be sorted.

It seemed I had become embroiled in a power struggle between two inspectors, and there was a difference of opinion as to what to do with me. The unfriendly inspector downstairs would have the final say, but now I had a better line of communication; something had changed. The following week, he told me he would let me know when there was a possibility of a test, so there was no point in waiting that day.

Then after a few days more of trying, the day came.

I was told in the morning to come back at 1.45 pm. I had my final lesson and waited patiently, hopefully for the last time. Then the examiner, after completing the paperwork, announced he wasn't feeling well and wouldn't be able to complete the exam. As he left, I was more concerned for my own situation than about his welfare. How many more hurdles would I have to overcome? However, he soon came back saying he felt better and we could continue.

First comes a yard test comprising a hill start, reversing and cornering. Failure at this stage means the end of the test. I passed with flying colours and was through to the next stage.

As we were driving around the area, the examiner started talking to me about my guiding. 'Do you go up Chapman's Peak Drive?' he asked. 'Yes, I do,' I replied. He then proceeded to tell me of a man he knew who committed suicide by driving off the cliff. Not what I wanted to think about while I was trying to concentrate on my driving.

After one lap of the area the examiner cut short the test, and we returned to the Traffic Department. He had seen enough. I had passed and it was only 12 weeks since I'd started the process — not the 12 months I had feared.

I merrily applied for my PDP and was immediately hit with a shock: I needed a work permit! Either this had failed to sink in when I'd been told months before, or I hadn't been told at all. My jubilation was short-lived.

The whole work permit business is a bureaucratic nightmare. To get a work permit I need a job (and an employer). To get a job I need a PDP. To get a PDP I need a work permit. It's a vicious circle — but I got there!

I also needed a work permit to register as a guide. In the end, I decided to pay a consultant to obtain a work permit for me. That way I could have my PDP *and* my tour guide registration. The consultant advised that I would face many problems with the paperwork if I tried to do it myself. The rules keep changing and 'Home Affairs', the government body that deals with such claims, is not always helpful. I couldn't afford a delay if I got it wrong, as I was soon returning to the UK for six months. I wanted everything in place for when I returned the following October — and happily this is exactly what happened, thanks to some local help from a good friend who dealt with things in my absence.

Getting around

When I first returned to Cape Town I purchased a bicycle. Most things are within walking distance in the city and I can travel easily around the suburbs on a bike. It was also a way of keeping fit and with the good weather there was not much chance of getting caught in rain. The only thing to battle against was the wind, the south easterly 'cape doctor'.

A friend recommended a second-hand bike shop in town. The bike wasn't expensive nor was it in the best condition, but it was less likely to be stolen. Of course I locked it up wherever I went. I loved that bike. I cycled everywhere that year, even longer distances. Cycling is not common in South Africa, unless you are an enthusiast with all the gear. So I was a bit of a novelty cycling around the city as I did.

The following year I decided I needed a car. I left my bike and some personal belongings in storage in a friend's garage whilst I was in the UK. Before I flew out to Cape Town I e-mailed my friends and asked them to look out for a room to rent and a car. One friend, Jenny, said I could stay in her boyfriend's place as he had a room available and also would I like to buy *her* car? She wanted the money for a business venture and I could buy the car for six months as long as I sold it back to her before I returned to the UK.

The car arrangement worked out perfectly, and I was able to drive into the Winelands area and beyond where I couldn't have gone on a bike. I was also able to pick up friends which again I couldn't do on two wheels.

I still used the bike frequently and preferred cycling to work than driving. Having spent most of the day driving whilst guiding, it was a pleasant change to get on my bike and pedal home. On the odd occasion when I was called early in the morning to help out on a guide, I would leave home at peak time and the traffic outside was queuing from the house to where I worked. If I had driven I would have not been able to get there in such good time.

Where I first laid my head — life with the Duke

Finding a room to rent was less satisfactory. This period took me into a world where I had no experience and where hopefully I won't ever have to go again.

Jenny's boyfriend had to give the spare room I was hoping to use to a family friend who had turned up at short notice. But she said: 'Don't worry, I'll pick you up at the airport. We will make a plan,' she added, as the South Africans are fond of saying.

When I arrived, Jenny suggested a few options, none very permanent. So I was taken to meet Charles, a friend of theirs. It turned out that they didn't know Charles well, and the idea of helping me had only come up at the last minute — yet Charles was very helpful. When he said he was shortly off to visit Polsmoor Prison, where he was involved in some welfare work, he asked if I would like to come along. I had never been inside a prison before so I jumped at the chance.

Charles was a lawyer and had become involved in a few cases at the prison when he decided to help further by organising better welfare facilities for the inmates.

We went to see if the new plants had arrived for his garden.

Normally it takes a lot of bureaucracy to get into a prison but Charles was a bit of a celebrity and we drove straight in. It was late in the afternoon and all the inmates had already been locked in their cells. He showed me around quickly before we left. He also showed me the cell used by Nelson Mandela during the three or so years he spent there, after being transferred from Robben Island. It was a short visit which unfortunately failed to meet my expectations.

I stayed with Charles for about three weeks, while I looked for somewhere to live. He lived in Newlands, an exclusive area of Cape Town where many film directors and business people live. It's very leafy, with green parks and lovely houses. It's English in character, and there was always a strong smell of summer flowers in the street when I walked to the house. There is one road around the corner, one of the most beautiful in the area with its quaint houses, a small historic church and beautiful flowering bougainvillea draped over the walls. I often drove the tour bus down that road when I was picking up from The Vineyard Hotel nearby so that we could all enjoy the scenery.

Like most South Africans, Charles was extremely helpful. He showed me around, bought me food for the house and sometimes we ate out.

I realised that something was wrong when I noticed that Charles kept offering to take me to the local bar. I like the odd drink, especially if the pub or bar has some atmosphere or good beer, but I don't go because I *need* a drink and I am afraid that was how Charles saw it. He would be very subtle and I would find that on a shopping trip I would end up meeting him at a bar in the shopping centre — only to find he had been there for a while and was probably two double gins and tonic ahead of me. I found out he was a regular when one of the waiters quietly referred to him as 'Mr G&T'.

This was my first experience of living with an alcoholic. Charles is the nicest man you could meet and would do anything for anybody. We got on very well and he was especially helpful towards me with my guiding. He had also trained as a tour guide and insisted on giving me information on tours. He spent ages poring over his laptop copying information onto discs for me.

Charles kept referring to the house as being owned by 'His Lordship' and when I asked who that was he said it was Lord Macauley of Macauley. During other conversations he mentioned his own Dukedom. When I quizzed him further he told me he was the Duke of Roxborough. So I was living with English gentry!

He fooled me for a while, until I took it up with people who know him better and they confirmed it was all made up. It was something people did to amuse themselves in the bars.

Frustrating times

This was a frustrating time for me. I wanted to be able to plan for the next six months. I wanted my independence and Charles kept hanging around and suggesting doing things together. Initially, I would play along and wait for him to get ready, but soon I could see he was holding me back. He had a habit of getting up at ridiculous hours in the morning because he couldn't sleep and he would start on the whisky. By the time I got up he was already fast asleep, slumped in his dining room chair by the window with his laptop open on the little table before him.

One morning, after agreeing to leave together, it took him an hour and a half to get showered, dressed and to drink some coffee while I waited for him. I could have done so much in that time, it was very frustrating. As I was working that afternoon, the morning was precious to me and it had been frittered away. I was unable to do the things I had hoped to do and in the end I had to postpone my plans until the following day.

Charles mentioned that he didn't get on with his brother, and then he'd had a row with another man. Later he had been thrown out of a bar and wasn't speaking to one of his friends. After a while I realised he had had a disagreement with most people and I was beginning to see the common denominator! Charles was also depressing company as the conversations we had were very negative. Every time I had an idea he'd say: 'Oh, you don't want to do that.' I was feeling stifled.

There wasn't a great incentive to leave though, as Charles was happy with my company, I was a rent-free guest and he was leaving for a business trip shortly anyway and I could have his rented room. The downside was that the owner of the house was due to return from the UK any day. And he was an alcoholic too.

The other thing that frustrated me about staying with Charles was that I didn't have a key. I relied on him being home to let me in, and I didn't always know where he was. On one occasion I was pretty sure he was home, as his car was outside and he is not one to travel without his car. I couldn't get to the front door because of the security gate so I rang his mobile phone — only to hear it ringing in the house. In the end I found him asleep in his chair. He hadn't heard a thing.

It just shows how useful security is: that day I had to climb over the low level wall to get into the front garden. Charles had left the front door open to allow fresh air into the house and I knew the door grille had no lock in it. As I climbed over the wall past the sign saying 'protected by XYZ armed security', I wondered whether a neighbour might spot me and report me to the police or call the armed security company — but nothing happened.

On another occasion when there was no answer and no car either, I rang Jenny who suggested he might be at the local hostelry. This turned out to be correct. I felt bad about dragging him out but he said he was just leaving. Actually it was a good move for him, as he was in no condition to drive. I put my bike in the back and drove him and his car home.

The broken whisky glass

I made up my mind to leave one morning after another incident. I was in bed dozing when I heard a smash. There wasn't any further disruption so I went back to sleep. Later, when I came into the lounge, heading for the bathroom, I saw Charles sitting at his chair with a bandage around his finger. 'I dropped a glass, drying up,' he declared. He assured me he was fine, so I carried on with my shower. In the bathroom I could see where he had attempted to clear up blood, lots of it, from the mess still on the floor. When I was dressed I wiped the surfaces down. There was blood everywhere.

Coming back into the lounge I again asked Charles if he was all right. He said he was — but then I saw the now red cloth around his hand and the pool of blood on the tiled floor where he had been dripping. The blood must have been there for a while as it had partially congealed. Blood had also splattered over his laptop and dried among the keys.

Without further argument I took him to the sink to clean the wound. It was a deep cut and the bleeding would not stop. How long had he been like that? As I removed the blood-soaked cloth from his hand a jet of blood spurted from his finger up the wall and over the sink and tiled splashback. I quickly rinsed his finger under the tap and then pinched the wound to stem the flow.

Now I regretted interfering, because I came over all hot and lightheaded at the sight of so much blood. I had to lean over the sink myself until I felt better. It took me a few minutes and sips of cool water to recover before bandaging the cut finger. Amazingly, Charles remained oblivious to it all, as if he hadn't injured himself in the slightest.

I spent ages clearing up the rest of the blood that day, and tidying up. Charles refused to go to hospital for a stitch, as I suggested, although he was very good at keeping the bandage on, not using his right hand and allowed me to re-dress the wound over the next few days. After that incident he was grateful for what I had done and he couldn't do enough for me.

Charles was also a smoker. I came home one day to find the window behind his chair broken. He told me he'd fallen through it but I suspect he was trying to empty his ashtray out of the window. I had seen him do it on numerous occasions before and there was a pile of cigarette ends outside, but this time the window must have been closed and he hadn't noticed so he had put his hand through the glass.

There were too many disasters waiting to happen in that house. I couldn't stay.

The problem with alcoholics is that they are in denial. They are constantly covering up their addiction even though everybody knows what is going on. They do not take responsibility for things and blame everyone else. Charles had a very short fuse; he was aggressive and had a negative outlook. I was unwilling to become a martyr to Charles, even though I felt sorry for his situation. As it turned out, he was moving on to pastures new anyway.

Charles wasn't working. He had not done any legal work for a while. He was in negotiation with some businessmen about flying to Lagos to start developing three hotels. He was to manage the development and was just waiting for the OK before he was off. The only problem was that he didn't trust the Nigerians and sensibly wanted certainty that his fare would be paid before he left. In fact they were going to book the flight and inform him of his departure time. This was to be in a few days so he needed to pack. As he was to be away for at least three months, or possibly up to two years, he was putting everything he wasn't taking with him into storage. He was moving out.

Charles would spend hours sitting in his chair by the window waiting for the call from Lagos. He must have spent a fortune calling these men on their mobiles. As a result he couldn't plan anything or get on with his life. It was obviously a strain for him, and this probably fuelled his drinking. After seeing him like this, getting more and more fed up and criticising the Nigerians, I asked him how long this had been going on. 'Since May,' he said — and that was in October. I couldn't believe it! No wonder the poor chap was fed up.

In the end I persuaded him to do something about it. 'How much longer are you going to sit around waiting for that call while your life passes you by?' I asked him. Eventually, he bit the bullet and flew to Lagos at his own expense to sort it all out. I took him to the airport and I also left his house the same day. I never heard whether there was a job for him or not.

After a few false starts I eventually found a place to stay in the Rondebosch area of Cape Town, not far from Charles's house. For six months I stayed in a self-contained flatlet in the garden of a large house, where I was given perfect privacy. Unfortunately, the couple who owned the property were not the friendliest or most helpful people I have met in South Africa — but they did leave me alone.

Living in Rondebosch enabled me to cycle to work, which also helped with my fitness.

I guided 88 tours that season. I found that I liked guiding and enjoyed the variety of animals, people and events happening all around me. I didn't need to guide in the townships again.

Back to the Township Tour — legacy of apartheid

The people from these townships often have menial jobs. In South Africa, there is no such thing as 'self service' at a garage as a petrol pump attendant provides necessary work. I made the mistake once of asking a pump attendant for directions, as you would in the UK. I was met with a blank look and was passed to another colleague. At first, I thought perhaps he didn't understand my accent, but now I realise he really didn't know. I fared no better with the second attendant and eventually gave up.

I wondered if this was because he didn't want to learn — however, I was told it is because these people haven't travelled far from their place of work. They will live in a shack nearby and will work seven days a week, only a street away from their home. They earn very little and have no resources to travel. The reason they didn't know the place I was seeking is because it's unlikely they had ever been there!

This all stems from the apartheid era when blacks were not educated at all — and with the best will in the world, it will take many generations to bring them up to speed.

Another low paid job is that of the security guard. Someone told me a trick recently that if I am in a hurry and want to park my car, I just tell them I have a meeting. I tried it at a big hotel here in Cape Town and suddenly, I became important and I was given a free parking space in their underground car park!

Origins of the township folk

Having visited the townships and the District Six Museum, I was drawn to learn more about the roots of these people. Where had they come from? There were those who came from the migrations of black people from central Africa and many of them, of course, were forcibly brought here as slaves in the seventeenth and eighteenth century.

The black people migrated from central Africa in about the 1400s. They were known as the Nguni people. Over time, various tribes established themselves in their own areas with much integration and change over the centuries. Today, we have nine black nations in South Africa, the diversity of which is mirrored in its eleven official languages. Apart from Afrikaans and English, there are nine black languages: Zulu, Xhosa, Sotho, Venda, Tswana, Tsonga, Pedi, Shangaan and Ndebele.

Life as a slave

Being a slave at the Cape meant a very hard life. Much depended on who owned you. Slaves were generally treated harshly. Owners considered them objects and the law confirmed this.

Many of the male slaves were skilled tradesmen, working as bricklayers, masons, carpenters, tailors or fishermen. Some were lucky and became grooms, coachmen, valets and butlers in households. Most did menial tasks such as working in the quarries, on farms, or in the gardens.

Tourists visiting Cape Town would not necessarily be aware that it was slaves who constructed the basic infrastructure and built the elaborate Cape Dutch buildings that survive today. Slaves were instrumental in building up the fruit and vegetable industries among others in the country.

The Malay flavours of the delicious dishes available now at Cape Town's tables have origins in the slave trade.

Female slaves were mainly domestic workers such as cooks, cleaners, nurses and washer women. They had a level of comfort, living and working in the homes of their owners. They tended the sick and dying, and were intimately associated with the family they served — often suckling the young of white mothers or providing sexual services to the men in the household.

Slaves faced many hardships. They worked long hours without breaks or holidays. Children were taken away from their parents and families were often split and sold off to different owners. It was humiliating to be sold like cattle at auction. They lost their identity and they were given new names by their owners — often religious names from the bible such as Susanna, Miriam, Jacob and Abraham, or they might be named after the month in which they were purchased.

Freedom of movement was curtailed because passes were compulsory. The carrying of lamps was required after dark and slaves were not allowed to wear shoes. Bare feet were a trademark of slavery.

Many colonists feared their slaves. With the large numbers in existence it would not have been difficult for a group to rise and cause havoc. This was the main reason slaves were suppressed and uneducated, as it took only one ring leader to start a rebellion. In all its history of slavery, it is surprising that there were only two uprisings at the Cape, both unsuccessful.

Resistance to slavery

Slaves showed their anguish and sense of hopelessness at being contained by running amok and inflicting indiscriminate injury or damage.

For example, a slave named January admitted attacking another slave, Moses, in a jealous rage in 1797. January was scourged, put in irons and sent to labour on the public works for twelve months. He was also kept in irons for a further four years and forbidden to appear in public until his sentence had expired.

Pilfering was favoured by female domestic slaves as a form of protest. In 1831 a slave named Deborah, who had more freedom than most slaves, for she worked for a bread and biscuit maker, stole handkerchiefs. She later returned to take thirty six silver thimbles, twelve muslin collars, nine pairs of silk gloves and twelve pairs of leather gloves. She was sentenced to three years imprisonment in the House of Correction.

Punishment was harsh, particularly in the early years of slavery. Flogging was commonplace for trivial misdemeanours such as impertinence, slovenliness, disregarding orders, neglecting one's work or quarrelling. Some slaves were put in stocks; women had their hair cut or were slapped or kicked.

Only after the arrival of the British in 1806 were some of the harshest punishments abolished.

'The execution… was the most cruel that could be invented by the art of man: a lingering death upon the rack, with the application of burning instruments in a manner too shocking to repeat.' This was how a 23-year-old named Jemima Kindersley recorded one such event during her visit in 1764. You can read more about her visit and other slave stories in 'Echoes of Slavery' by Jackie Loos.

I was carrying out some additional research for this book in the UK, reading a book on slavery as I commuted by train into London. One day, I was standing in the aisle of a packed early morning train when I came to the part about a slave being punished in this horrible manner. I was reading about the Reverend Samuel Broadbent of the Wesleyan Missionary Society, who in 1825 witnessed the horrifying way in which corporal punishment was received in public by slaves and people of colour.

He reported on a number of criminals, who were punished with public flogging and branding for diverse offences. It was when he went into detail about the state of the back of this particular slave during the flogging, which I won't repeat, that I began to feel ill on the train. I was glad to get off the train to take in some fresh air.

The smallpox epidemic of 1755 was a devastating outbreak which affected the white population as much as the slaves. Jemima Kindersley attributed the disease to the poor physical condition of the colonists, whom she described as being 'mostly fat gross people' as a result of a diet that included 'vast amounts of grease and butter'.

Slaves were illiterate, having received little or no education from their owners. Educating slaves became a duty of the missionaries who also saw an opportunity to convert the slaves to their religion.

In later years slaves complained to the fiscal, the courts and the slave protectors about their mistreatment. Often the fiscal and the courts, if they investigated at all, upheld the owner's story and the slave faced even more ill treatment as the owner took vengeance when the slave returned.

Illiterate slaves used the services of notaries (people with some legal training) if they couldn't write themselves. Sometimes the notary was unable to explain the issue clearly or had a habit of using inappropriate words or phrases that upset the fiscal, leaving the slaves with no chance of winning.

In the case of slave Joris, Wilhelm Gebhart, owner of the wine estate Simonsvlei in Paarl, became the first European to be executed for the death of a slave. Young Wilhelm Gebhart had recently taken over ownership of the farm with responsibility for the many slaves at Simonsvlei. One day in September 1822, he rode out into the fields where the slaves were working and was told by the supervisor that Joris was malingering and had already been beaten twice to no avail. Young Gebhart became incensed and ordered Joris to be beaten again, this time with bundles of quince branches. The beating continued when they returned to the farm, and salt and vinegar were rubbed into the wounds to increase his agony. After 139 strokes, the slave was found dead in his bed the next morning.

Testimony from one slave who walked to town to raise the alarm, and later that of others too, was sufficient to condemn the accused. Despite many requests for a reprieve, Wilhelm Gebhart, aged 22, was hanged in November 1822.

Buying your freedom
The only reward slaves could look forward to was 'manumission' (being made a free person). Some slaves were manumitted by their white owners in return for good service. If a master fell in love with a female slave she had to be manumitted

before marriage because slaves were banned from inter-racial marriages.

Freedom was not always a happy arrangement. Free persons had to find a home, feed themselves and their family, as well as find work. Often people would end up in hire houses in the poorer area of the city as they struggled to find their way in a hostile world.

Slaves were often manumitted when the estate of a deceased was settled. One such woman, Romina, found her joy of freedom short lived. Her two daughters continued as slaves as she could not afford the money to free them. Romina was separated from her children and even on Sundays her daughters were not permitted to visit their mother. The governor refused to intervene and it wasn't until four years after Romina died that the girls received their freedom.

In 1828 a group of worthy businessmen and clergy started 'The Cape of Good Hope Philanthropic Society', whose purpose was to aid deserving slaves and slave children to purchase their freedom. The society raised funds to purchase children aged three to ten, to be apprenticed until they were sixteen with masters or mistresses as approved by the committee.

Many people saw this gesture as an alternative form of slavery.

Slavery at the Cape ended on 1st December 1834. Slaves were prevented from enjoying their instant freedom, by being required to serve a four-year compulsory apprenticeship until 1838. Most slaves had expected immediate emancipation and were bitterly disappointed to have to wait a further four years. Employers were supposed to prepare their slaves for freedom during this apprenticeship period, but few of them bothered. Indeed, some employers saw the probation period as a problem too, as they were burdened with supporting troublesome employees for a further four years.

After 1838, ex-slaves became free to choose where to work and as a result previously harsh employers found it difficult to find labour. Ex-employers were compensated for their losses by the government.

Celebrating in Cape Town

On the first and second of January each year, Cape Town throws a carnival to celebrate the emancipation of slaves. The local coloureds themselves call it the 'Coon Carnival'. This is a particularly festive affair and I make a point of being in the area so I don't miss it.

Endorsed by Nelson Mandela in 1996, 'The Coon Carnival' or 'The Cape Minstrel Carnival' has roots in the eighteenth century when slaves were given their one day off in the year, the second of January. On this day, dozens of bands snake along a pre-determined route from the District Six side of the city to the stadium at Green Point, where they all congregate in the open car park.

It's a photographer's dream to be situated along the route, with numerous opportunities to snap the bands as they pass. Everybody is happy and cheering as the minstrels, wearing their brightly coloured nylon suits and displaying elaborately painted faces parade by. Many of them sing and dance up close to me. It's impossible to avoid being swept up in the fever of the moment. Trumpeters show off, bass drummers bash and youngsters dance as they parade along the crowded streets in the sunshine. It's a wonderful sight, so many coloured people celebrating in this way, and everybody having fun.

The bands spend all year preparing for this spectacle, making uniforms in their chosen colours and practising their unique tunes. Much is at stake as the winning band will be awarded a large sum of money.

I enjoy going to Green Park Stadium to be among the groups and enjoy the carnival atmosphere as the bands continue their parade around the ground. It's a chance to get some good 'up front' photographs and to catch participants off-guard as they relax after the procession.

When I found out that Joe, one of the managers of District Six Museum, has his own band, I was interested to hear him. After a few false starts my girlfriend and I did get to see him play. Joe is coloured and his band played at a prestigious hotel in Contantia. It was a joy to hear them play an enormous variety of jazzy music that night. He has a sweet, melodious voice and the band was excellent.

Whilst slavery was not a noble thing, it did provide opportunities for some illiterate non-religious people. Certainly, the colonists benefited and the growth of the Cape would not have been the same had slaves not been imported. Its legacy is still very real today, with the influence on the culture, cuisine, language and religion, without which Cape Town would not be so vibrant today.

... What did I learn?

Say 'yes' and find a way to do it afterwards — trust that it will work out. When you don't get the right answer to your question, try asking someone else. Never say 'no' to an opportunity; you can always get something from the experience. When you have failed a test, there is usually a good reason; review your failings before trying again.

Taking action gets results — it's better to try things than to worry and do nothing. Your situation can change very rapidly and you can soon master another challenge in no time at all.

Think of hurdles as 'challenges' and your outlook will take on a new meaning.

Chapter 6
The Kwazulu-Natal Tour

I have travelled through KwaZulu-Natal (KZN) on a number of occasions and I always enjoy visiting this province. I don't guide in this area, but if I were to extend my guiding knowledge this is the next province I would choose.

Much of KZN's countryside consists of green rolling hills much like the British countryside. The climate is sub-tropical, unlike the Mediterranean climate of Cape Town. In KZN they get their rainfall in the summer and the best time to see game is in winter when water is scarcer and animals have to move to water holes to drink. Also the vegetation is higher in summer which makes it more difficult to view animals. They simply disappear into the undergrowth.

South Africa's best-known city, Durban, is in KZN. KZN has fantastic beaches, the Hluhluwe-Umfolozi Game Reserve, The Greater St Lucia Wetlands Park, the stunning Drakensberg

Mountains, the Battlefields and the Midlands area, as well as other coastal regions north and south of Durban.

My favourite entertainment in Durban is the uShaka Aquarium, part of uShaka Sea World. Named after Shaka, the great Zulu warrior, the uShaka is the best aquarium I have visited. It is housed in an old steam ship which has been renovated to look like a wreck. You enter the aquarium through a hole in the side of the ship, well below the water line. Inside are remnants of the old ship: tea chests, old rope, existing signs to obsolete hatches and doors. You really get the feel of being in an old ship as you wander around fish tanks viewing the many varieties of fish they contain.

When a group of us came to Durban from God's Golden Acre, (which I will come to later), for a night out, we had dinner on the 'Top Deck' of the ship. I was pleased to see the care that the local police took when eight of us arrived in town for a night out and, finding only fast food restaurants, we asked a passing patrol where they would recommend that we eat. They suggested the uShaka, and then offered to escort us there. Durban is still trying to overcome certain 'no-go' areas with new development. Between uShaka and the many beaches is an area called The Point which is yet to be lifted from its past, and unsuspecting visitors should avoid it.

Having parked some way from our location, the police gave us a lift to uShaka on their 'bakkie' (open-backed truck) which delighted the group enormously. Then the police introduced us to a security guard who was able to take us to the Top Deck restaurant where we enjoyed an evening of great food, wine and entertainment.

I was pleased to see the police making an effort as they are often condemned for their lack of effectiveness. They clearly didn't want something bad to come of us.

On safari

Deep in Zululand is the Hluhluwe-Umfolozi Game Park, one of the most popular game parks in the world. I have visited this park a number of times, mostly the Hluhluwe section (pronounced 'shushloowee' or as near as I can get to the Zulu pronunciation). Both reserves were established as long ago as 1895 and are now combined to form one single park.

Hluhluwe is well-known for its diversity of flora and fauna amongst densely forested lowlands to open hill summits cut by the deep valley of the Hluhluwe River which has given the place its name. Hluhluwe contains a large range of animals and is the only reserve where I have seen 'The Big Five' in one night.

The Big Five consists of the lion, the leopard, the rhino, the buffalo and the elephant. In colonial times when hunters hunted game, these were the most prized trophies. They were the most dangerous animals and therefore the most difficult to kill.

The leopard is the most difficult of the Big Five to see. They are often found lying in the branches of a jacaranda tree — so, if you want to see a leopard, look for a jacaranda tree. Often, the leopard will hang his catch of impala on a branch until he is hungry.

Black or white? — that is the question

The Umfolozi is one of the most important sanctuaries in the world for the protection of the white (square-nosed) rhino. This species was once on the verge of extinction due to excessive ivory poaching and is now flourishing thanks to the careful management of the reserve. The park now exports white rhino to other sanctuaries and zoos all over the world, thus maintaining a constant number of animals believed to be sustainable for the size of the park.

Both the black and the white rhino are dark grey-brown in colour and not black or white at all like their names. These came about because of a mis-pronounciation by Europeans. The white rhino was originally called the square-lipped or wide-lipped rhino whereas the black rhino was called the hook-lipped rhino because of its obvious lip distinction. The Europeans misheard 'wide' for 'white' and called it the white rhino. It was then logical to call the other species the black rhino.

There have been many initiatives to reduce poaching over the years and none has been successful — nor will they be, as long as men in the Far East believe that the grinding of horn into powder enhances their libido. Now it seems that Viagra is becoming the best means to reduce the worldwide poaching of ivory.

My most frightening experience with a rhino was when I was on a wilderness safari in Umfolozi. We rounded a bush and the guide in front suddenly told us to back up. There was a rhino there, a female with her young calf. The worst situations in which to confront a wild animal are head-on, and when the animal has a baby — and we had done both.

It was all the more exciting because I had been feeling disappointed at having seen no wildlife at all that day, and was thinking we had made a mistake in joining a group that was more interested in talking and smoking than in viewing animals.

Before we could understand from the back of the line what was happening, we were warned that the animal was charging. At the start of the walk we had been briefed what to do in the event of danger from various wild animals. When charged by a rhino it is best to climb a tree, but that is not always the first thing that crosses your mind. As I ran back, rather half-heartedly, my first thought was that it would be a great story to tell my mates at home, not that I should climb a tree to avoid the danger.

Then, it all went quiet. I looked over my shoulder expecting it to be all over — instead, I found myself eyeball-to-eyeball with the rhino. It seemed to be just staring at me, snorting and pawing the ground with its hoof. Then it charged again, and this time it was serious. Here I was, on the ground at the mercy of this huge animal that can weigh up to 1.6 tonnes for a female, run at speeds of 35mph and turn on a sixpence. Everyone ran in different directions. I ran straight through a gorse bush with what looked like 30-millimetre needles; others climbed trees. The ranger and the Zulu-speaking guide both fired their guns across the path of the rhino, and she diverted off and eventually disappeared.

To remove my hat, which was now embedded in the middle of the gorse bush, the ranger risked injuring his arm. I had run straight through this bush, emerging with hardly a scratch, with so much adrenalin exploding through my veins!

Some years later, a ranger died in similar circumstances when he was trampled to death by a charging rhino, having met it after walking around a bush. I am lucky to be alive.

Had I not survived, I would never have understood the value of contribution!

CONTRIBUTION

There comes a time in your life when you realise that something isn't quite right. You have been working hard all your life, you have a loving family with great friends, yet there is still something missing.

Slowly, many people come to realise that *contribution* is the missing link. Giving something back to the community gives you a sense of satisfaction, of completeness, of being worthy. *I came into this by accident*, you might say, or *was I being led by a greater power*?

Either way, I started to think there must be more to life. I was ready to do something about it.

Becoming a coach

My first encounter with the charity called 'God's Golden Acre' happened in 2005. It was a Landmark Education course in which I had participated back in 2001, only this time I was one of the coaches.

Becoming a coach had been a long-held dream, and I had a gap in my diary when someone from the programme invited me to take part in the Self Expression and Leadership course. I was to coach six participants, who would organise their own project in the community. I would have my own coach too, who in turn would be coached by the course leader. In this way, everybody gets support and the system works really well.

My students' projects included a musical performance in a local park in London, a street party in London, a children's sports day near Manchester and a charity fun run near London.

Being a coach, I have learned that you have to be firm with coachees. Being kind all the time is more in my nature — but as a coaching technique it is counterproductive. In effect, it lets the client off the hook instead of stretching him or her, so there is less benefit. I've had to learn to be tougher.

There were over 60 participants on the course, with 13 coaches and a leader. That would lead to more than 75 projects in the community. Imagine the impact that will have on all those communities and individuals — from just one course!

Being a coach this time, I also had to have a project. Landmark's view was that I could not inspire people to be successful in their projects unless I had one running in parallel, which I found to be true.

So, aiming high, I thought back to a time a few years before when I'd been researching for a similar project that I didn't pursue. My idea had been to help underprivileged children in a foreign country. Was this the time to make it happen?

My coach prompted me to consider a project related to my visit to South Africa later that year. What would it be like if the people of that country were expecting me when I arrived? I believed the idea to be beyond my capabilities, and that I was unworthy of such an accolade — yet it inspired me. And that is exactly what did happen.

I thought about children in South Africa, and AIDS came to mind. So, I rang AIDS Africa in South Africa. When I described my construction skills and tourism experience to their representative, she told me about Heather Reynolds, who did good work with children, and gave me the telephone number of God's Golden Acre (GGA).

When I called GGA I spoke to Rebecca, the then General Manager. When I explained my skills and background she said they wanted to expand their building programme. So I said: 'I will do it!' That was how it all started.

God's Golden Acre

Heather has devoted her life to helping children in KwaZulu-Natal where AIDS is prevalent. It's her calling from God, she says. Heather believes strongly that God has given her this task. She is doing it extraordinarily well.

She speaks fluent Zulu, having been brought up with Zulu people, and she also speaks Norwegian.

This is a woman who makes things happen, often in situations where others have previously failed. She has slowly built up God's Golden Acre from its infancy in 1995, through near-bankruptcy, to be the thriving organisation that it is today.

Some organisations have a large budget and defined structure, but Heather's philosophy is to not concentrate efforts in one area. She will be there for any child who needs help, which often means spreading herself and GGA thinly.

This is how GGA describes itself on its website:

God's Golden Acre Khayelihle is a non profit making charity involved in the care of children who have been orphaned or abandoned because of HIV/AIDS related illness and violence.

Rather than simply putting the children in orphanages, God's Golden Acre Khayelihle primarily strives to keep children in their community setting by assisting families using various initiatives to support themselves.

Their aim is to achieve the following:

- *To provide children with a good education*

- *To assist them to become well-adjusted adults*

- *To develop the natural talents and aptitudes of each and every child*

- *To provide a caring, loving, nurturing and compassionate community environment*

Although most people link God's Golden Acre Khayelihle with residential care, the majority of the work is done in the rural areas that have been devastated by HIV/AIDS in KwaZulu-Natal, South Africa.

God's Golden Acre Khayelihle's aim is to develop communities to create sustainable means for children to care for themselves and to rebuild their communities.

The enormity of the HIV situation needs a holistic approach between different agencies and like-minded organisations. With this in mind God's Golden Acre Khayelihle does the following work:

Based in Cato Ridge, this is an outreach project that cares for, at present 5,000 children in extended families in the rural areas. Older sibling and granny headed families have become so impoverished that they are finding it increasingly difficult to provide for their children. Lack of infrastructure - no running water facilities, electricity, fuel or employment opportunities - makes it more difficult for them to cope. Failing health and almost non-existent medical facilities further add to the seriousness of the situation.

The aims of the outreach programme are:

Impact Migration

- *to meet the immediate needs of these families through food, schooling and housing. This includes monthly parcels, pre-school, school fees, school uniforms and stationery, and the maintenance or building of secure houses*

African Sporting Academy

- *the God's Golden Acre Khayelihle Sporting Academy provides rehabilitation and empowerment programmes using sport*

Arts and Culture Academy

- *crafts, drama, song and dance provide rehabilitation and empowerment programmes and positive environments where children can work through very difficult and challenging experiences*

Arts and Skills Development

- *to strengthen families' capacity to cope by implementing stimulating, innovative and practical solutions so that they may eventually become self-sufficient. This can be achieved through providing life-skills, training, agricultural and skills training, and business training*

HIV/AIDS incidences are starting to slow down in the area, with currently 230 people per day dying of AIDS-related illnesses in the valleys around GGA. People spend much of their time going to funerals, and this has a huge impact on their lives — not to mention the effect of others around them who are very ill.

The houses we build are simple, comprising concrete block walls on a concrete foundation, a corrugated tin roof strapped to timbers, metal windows and an external door. The walls are sealed inside and out with a slurry coat, and decorated inside with emulsion. Internal doors are often left off; people prefer to use curtains because doors waste space in small surroundings. Electricity, to supply a few bulbs for lighting, is often installed later. People cook with propane gas in the kitchen. Water is supplied to a stand-pipe to a local point in the vicinity and each house is provided with a government issue portable toilet requiring a long drop.

We have also started building proper pre-schools for the local communities.

My course project

The aim of my project, as far as the course was concerned, was to find five volunteers and raise £2,500 in the three months' duration of the course. Towards the end of the three months I set aside half an hour a day and telephoned all the South African banks in London and all the South African companies I could think of in the UK.

I had previously learned to cold-call during my business years, so it wasn't too difficult to pick up the phone, speak to strangers and ask them for money. I just tell them what I am doing and how great it is to be able to help children who are in need, and people are generally willing to hear my story.

The difficulty was that companies get requests from people all the time and they have to filter out so many of them. Most companies now have a sponsorship contribution policy, and adopt a charity to support each year with an annual budget. They often encourage community days for their employees to take part in, which may be related to local communities rather than in 'far-off South Africa'.

In the end, I didn't manage to raise the sponsorship from these companies. But I not only succeeded in my project for the course — I exceeded it.

Volunteering

I started looking around for volunteers and I told everybody I met about my project. We also shared our experiences and progress with the other coaches on the course — all 13 of them.

One day, another coach called Kellie was meeting her best friend after an evening session, and I happened to meet her in the corridor of Landmark. She said: 'Nick, tell my friend Ania about your project. She is very interested.' A few days later, Ania called: 'Could we meet up for a drink and discuss your project more? I'd really like to do this!' That was just the start, because Ania began inspiring her own friends to join her in a volunteer group.

Meanwhile, I used my contacts in the construction industry to generate interest in the project. It seemed logical to talk to construction companies about building, even in another country.

One day, I happened to make contact with the right man. Mainly I was interested in sponsorship — but

I happened to mention that I needed volunteers too. George was the director responsible for the company's graduate programme and offered construction graduates for my volunteering. He could see a benefit in his graduates going over to South Africa to do this work and was prepared to consider funding the project. 'Send me more details,' he said.

Following a meeting and a series of telephone conversations the scheme was approved. Multiplex, the Australian developer and construction company, became my first construction volunteer group. At the time, they employed 30 graduates in the UK and others in Australia, New Zealand and the Middle East. Multiplex are now known as Brookfield Construction.

Had I just asked George for sponsorship, I might have got nothing at all. Because I had mentioned volunteering, I got many volunteers *and* the whole sponsorship as well. It is worth communicating everything, even if it's not your original intention.

Multiplex agreed to provide ten graduates and fund their flights. The graduates were asked to raise sponsorship for the cost of the building materials, about £250 per person. This they did by asking their contractors to contribute. Some of Multiplex's suppliers and contractors wanted to know more about how to get involved in this worthwhile project.

In the end, two graduates resigned and there was insufficient time to replace them, so only eight graduates joined me at GGA in March 2006.

We agreed to finish off an accommodation block for GGA, which involved fitting out the block with showers, toilets, fixed beds and all the internal and external joinery, suspended ceilings and decorations. In addition, we laid the foundations for the home, to be built by Ania and her group.

When it came to asking people for help I felt as if I were dumping on them, and being a nuisance — but I soon realised that people generally had sympathy for what I was doing. Even if they couldn't help, they would wish me luck. In other cases, people came up to me and offered money or asked how they could help. I was blown away. It wasn't difficult to get help and that spurred me on.

It was as if I were kindling a locked-up desire to help others in the world. Many people empathise with the plight of children, as I do. Some of them can't help directly but are willing to sponsor us in our project. One good friend of mine, Vicky, thanked me for the opportunity to sponsor us. She could not help physically but was willing to sponsor us when I asked.

People gain such a lot from going to GGA. They learn about the problems in KwaZulu-Natal, and realise how lucky we are to be born in a western society with so many opportunities and relative wealth. In the UK we have the welfare state to fall back on if all else fails. This is not so available in Africa.

They also learn to stretch themselves, and to take on challenges bigger than they believe possible. They raise sponsorship in their own community, in their own way, and achieve a lot in a short time.

Ania had set about talking to her friends and forming a group of ten volunteers. She was sure she would be able to get only a small group together — but I had more faith in her than she did herself! Over a period of months she found all ten volunteers, mainly from the entertainment industry.

For funding, Ania and her friends set up a website called www.homesofhope.org.uk. They raised all their sponsorship through this website, which also gave information about their project. Later, it detailed their achievements on a day to day basis. They flew out to GGA in April 2006.

The house they built was in Mopelo, for a 13 year old boy called Mthobisi, who was living under a tin roof. Heather was concerned that he might stray into bad habits if he was not helped soon. He had a younger sister and Heather hoped that they would be looked after by a member of their extended family. In time, other children would probably join them in this house. Mthobisi is currently on GGA's food drop programme.

Later in 2006, two South Africans, Salomé and Barbara, contacted me through the Homes of Hope website. They were living and working in London at the time. Over the coming months they succeeded in bringing together 14 volunteers from many countries including Germany, Italy, Poland and the UK.

I was there for the first week to settle them into God's Golden Acre.

The house they helped to build in March 2007 was for a boy called Menzi. He came from a family up on the hill overlooking the Sanconscha valley. Heather told us his heartbreaking story when we visited her just after the group arrived in March.

Menzi's house

Heather told us about the people living on the hill opposite GGA's base who had a reputation in the community. They were a totally dishevelled bunch: dirty, poor and totally disinterested in a society that had rejected them. There were women who had become prostitutes — nobody but their clients ever went up there.

One day a little girl appeared in the valley. The girl had an arm behind her back which Heather thought might be holding something. The girl reluctantly revealed her hand and to Heather's surprise her palm contained an abscess the size of an egg. The little girl pleaded: 'Please don't say anything or I will get into trouble.'

Heather decided she must go up the hill, find the girl's mother and get permission to take her to hospital. And off she went.

When she got there, she found women dressed in rags, lying around either drunk or high on drugs. They threw cold hostile looks at her, which made Heather afraid, and hissed: 'We don't need you do-gooders here. Go away!' There didn't appear to be many men around. She got out of the car with the little girl beside her. There were many children scurrying around and Heather saw the poor condition they were in. They all had ringworm and practically no hair. They also had scabies with terrible sores on their bodies.

Heather went up to the women and asked which one was the girl's mother. Nobody spoke, so Heather asked again. The little girl went over to one lady whom Heather assumed was her guardian. Heather immediately asked her about her daughter. 'This girl has got huge sores and her blood may be poisoned. Can I have your permission to take her to hospital?' The lady didn't reply.

'If I don't take this girl to hospital now, her blood could be poisoned, her kidneys could be unable to cope with it and fail, because that is what happens,' Heather persisted. 'She will be very ill and will probably die. Do you want her to die?' Eventually, the lady waved her head in some form of agreement. So Heather took the girl to hospital where she was put on a drip. Then the girl convalesced with Heather for a while, and slowly recovered.

Heather obtained an enormous container of ringworm treatment from an Australian doctor friend. She went back up the hill and started applying the treatment to the children's heads, and scabies ointment to treat their skin. She avoided the cold and hostile eyes of the women. Over a period of time, the children's hair started to grow back healthily and their skin condition improved.

In subsequent years, Heather supported the families with monthly food parcels and the children started attending school with GGA paying their fees and providing their uniforms.

One day, many years later, Heather visited again with the community health worker and it was arranged that she would bring fruit trees. She had already brought some chickens. All the community had been asked to do was dig the holes for the fruit trees — but they hadn't done a thing!

Heather was so furious, she spoke to the community health worker and threatened: 'I've had it with this lot. They don't want to do a thing to help themselves. I am going to take these fruit trees and the chickens back with me.'

Suddenly, the women reacted. They said: 'Give us ten minutes. We will dig the holes.'

'Ok! Ten minutes,' Heather replied — and they were galvanised into action. She told us later that she had never seen people move so fast.

Then, to her amazement, some of the women brought her a bench to sit on. The children gathered round, very affectionately — after all, she had spent a lot of time with these children over the years. While Heather waited for the tree holes, she asked the children if they would sing a song with her. She started singing a song in English. Even though they couldn't understand the words, they soon got the hang of it and sang with her:

> *This little light of mine,*
> *I'm going to let it shine,*
> *This little light of mine,*
> *I'm going to make it shine.*

Once the holes were dug, the children sang the song to the adults. For the first time in years, Heather noticed there were no more hostile glares.

When she left the community that day, Heather was elated. She had changed the community. The change continued: the women dressed better, having recovered their self-respect. Of all the work she has done with many families over the years, the effort with this community has given her the most satisfaction.

Within this community, there was a boy then aged about 13 who was stealing. He came down to visit GGA and was caught stealing from the volunteers. Heather told him that she would help anyone out in the community, whoever they were, but she would not tolerate a person stealing around her. The boy kept coming back — but Heather reminded him about her rule. By now he was about 15. He said he could sing and dance and asked if he could join the choir. Heather again turned him away.

One day the young man came in while they were auditioning for new parts in their latest performance. It was the same person, but somehow very different. He was polite and had an air of confidence. He asked to audition for the choir. Heather had heard that he had a beautiful voice, and rather than prejudice the choir's view, she allowed them to make the decision. They allowed the boy to step up on the stage.

His audition was to sing a solo in his mother tongue — Zulu — and then a song in English, followed by a duet. He then had to finish with a dance. When the boy opened his mouth everyone was amazed how good his voice was. It was just breaking and had real depth.

Again, the choir was given the option of accepting him, as Heather was leaving on a tour the following day. When she came back a few weeks later she hadn't heard anything about the boy, but was surprised when she saw the choir again and found him already rehearsing with them.

Now the boy, Menzi, is 17, and seen as a role model by other members of his community. Heather hopes that other people in that community will see that by being honest they can progress and lift themselves out of their poor environment. Heather is training Menzi to be a leader of his community, and it is hoped that he will go to university. And so we started to build the house for Menzi.

Back in 2006, I had arrived with the Multiplex volunteers to build my first house. We had been told that the location of the site had been agreed only the day before. We arrived at the site, keen to set to work. As we unloaded the truck of equipment there was a lorry bearing sand standing by, waiting to unload.

The site was very uneven and we wondered why we couldn't use a digger, as we would in the UK. It would take two days to clear and level the site by hand, whereas a digger would have the work done in an hour or two. The answer is that the cost of hiring one for a day would pay for six men for two days. There is very little employment in the area, and if we used a machine the locals would be upset that we were not providing jobs; they would probably ransack the house later on. Any use of mechanical equipment has to be done sensitively, and often with the agreement of the local Zulu chief.

As we were discussing this issue, a few neighbours appeared from the next door property and questioned our presence there. One of the men, dressed in a wrap-around cloth and bare-chested, carried a menacing knife and looked none too pleased. It turned out that whilst someone representing the household had agreed with the house building, someone else had changed their mind and it was not to take place.

After a few phone calls we eventually decided not to aggravate the local community, and to start building at an alternative site in another part of the valley.

One year later, in 2007, I arrived with Salomé's group. On the first day of building we were driving a truck full of concrete blocks to our new site, and passed the piece of land where we'd nearly had trouble the previous year. Just down the road from that site we passed a group of locals. One of them looked familiar — and he was eyeing me, probably with the same thought. We both knew we had met before. He was the man with the large knife.

The food drop

I always tie in a food drop with the dates for building a house of hope. It gives the volunteers a wider understanding of the problems here and a chance to learn more about the culture. A Zulu man accompanies us to translate and explain.

The food is provided by sponsors. Many families are unable to feed themselves. Some are without parents. Neighbours are helpful in the short-term but may themselves have to go without in order to support others.

The government programme is available, but often the government is unaware of these people. To complete the paperwork to get on to a government programme takes time and involves proof of identity which is often difficult for people in the rural areas. The process can take a year — too long for hungry people to wait. So, non-government organisations such as GGA provide a service to distribute food parcels supplied by sponsors in the meantime.

On this occasion in 2007, we drove out to Tugela Ferry in the farthest valley from GGA's base at Cato Ridge. The first drop-off was for a family of three little boys and their mother. When we arrived the mother stepped out of the 'rondavel', a round Zulu hut made of sticks and mud. As we approached, the little boys appeared in the door opening. Two of the girls in our group wanted to take photographs and were invited into the rondavel by the mother — but inside it was too dark to see, there being no windows. It was a good example of how people live. The huts don't last very long and eventually crumble.

Nowadays, houses are being built with concrete blocks and a tin roof. Usually, the blocks are bought from a local merchant, but sometimes they are homemade from mud, with grass added for strength to save money compared with more modern products.

The second visit was to a boy who had no parents. As we approached, the boy, aged about 14, was walking home from school and pleased to see us. His house was built of mud and sticks, and the roof had been ripped off in a storm the previous night. The walls were so damaged that it would be difficult to re-fix the roof without extensive repairs. Sheets of corrugated tin lay stacked on the grass, weighed down under a few blocks.

Mr Mapanga, our Zulu interpreter, asked: 'Is there anyone who could help you with the roof?' and the boy replied: 'No.' So, Mr Mapanga made a call on his mobile phone and made sure some local people he knew would take action.

For the volunteers, who had not seen this part of Africa before, these were two very good examples of life in the rural areas and the girls were particularly moved by the experience.

It was interesting for me too, as I had never before been so close to the people in the villages. On my previous food drop I had helped with delivery to a central point, the community centre, where the families came to collect their food. Initially, I didn't think they could be very poor, judging by what they were wearing — but I was told these people wear their Sunday best for the occasion. The Zulus are a very proud people.

On this occasion, we set out the food parcels in thirteen rows of three. These parcels consist of three ten-kilogram sacks: one of maize, one of rice and one of beans. There will also be a small bag of goodies such as tea bags, soap, matches and other necessities, depending on the sponsor. The local people came along and each stood alongside a food parcel. Their card was punched, and as if someone had given the all-clear, they collected their food parcels and left. Wheelbarrows appeared from everywhere, sacks were lifted onto heads and the goods disappeared. I saw one woman carry three sacks on her head. That's thirty kilograms worth!

Today, we were making single drops to individual families, and we saw the homes they lived in and their environment. This was a far more revealing and realistic experience for everyone.

Tourists who visit South Africa see very little of life in these communities and don't always appreciate the hardships endured by the rural people. I am sure there is more I can do to raise that awareness whilst tourists are enjoying their holiday in the region.

Back to the KwaZulu-Natal Tour — lagoon life

A very different region from the Hluhluwe Game Reserve is the coastal region of St Lucia. The Greater St Lucia Wetlands Park, as it is properly called, is a mixture of lakes, lagoons, swamps, islands and high sand dunes. The little town of St Lucia is peaceful, with a number of lovely guesthouses and restaurants. It's a relaxing place to spend a few days.

The area was proclaimed a game reserve in 1897 and later enlarged to include the surrounding land. The reserve is home to many animals, particularly different types of buck. There is good fishing here and more than 350 species of birds. I have seen the African fish eagle here on each visit, as well as the amazingly bright blue malacite kingfisher and the mangrove kingfisher.

With over 70 hippos in the region it is not difficult to find this docile animal, which spends most of its day wallowing in the lagoon keeping cool, protecting itself from sunburn and biting insects. It becomes active at night when it comes ashore searching for food, sometimes walking miles in a single night. It can also be seen sunbathing on the banks during cool evenings. Surprisingly, this animal is the most dangerous wild mammal in Africa. If frightened on land, a hippo charges back to the safety of the water and anything in its way is likely to be trampled.

Whilst in the water, the hippo is a very enjoyable creature to watch as you pass by on one of the many boat safaris along the lagoon. They are often seen standing or lying on the bottom with just their ears, eyes and nostrils exposed. Babies use their parents as rafts in deep water.

If a boat gets too close, the dominant male will display a yawn, exposing his huge tusks as a warning to keep away. This is also an act of aggression to remind other males to leave his harem of females alone.

Crocodiles are also interesting to see, at a distance. They too bask in the sun on the banks of the lagoon, waiting while their body temperature rises before they become more active. They kill their victims by taking them under water and drowning them, spinning their poor victim to force air from their lungs. Crocodiles usually kill only when hungry — but have been known to attack large numbers of migrating wildebeest crossing a river, apparently just for fun.

The battle-hard Zulus who made KwaZulu-Natal

The Zulus emerged from the Nguni people, who migrated south from central Africa in the 1400s.

The Zulus make up the largest tribal group in South Africa, numbering almost eight million. Known for their prowess in war, the Zulus live in the valley of Zululand. The Zulu, meaning 'people of heaven', are a proud nation. They are friendly and hospitable, and treasure their heritage.

Shaka (1788-1828) was the most famous warrior of all. He trained the great Zulu warriors to be battle-hard and then took over other tribes in the area to expand his nation. His story is depicted in the film Zulu, featuring Michael Caine. Shaka was eventually murdered by his brother Dingane, who took over as king.

Beads are a very prominent feature of women's dress, with married women wearing head-dresses decorated with beads to denote their status. Every colour of bead carries a different meaning. Young Zulu girls, in particular, send sweet messages to their loved ones using the creative language of beads. Men wear skin aprons and fur armlets and anklets.

Zulus live in beehive huts formed in a circle known as a 'kraal'. The Zulus are renowned for their warrior-like behaviour, and their dances still reflect this today, with dancers armed with colourful shields and lots of spear waving.

In the Battlefields area, place names such as Rorke's Drift, Isandlwana, Dingane's Kraal and Spioenkop all relate to local battles.

One of the renowned battles of the Anglo-Zulu War took place at Isandlwana. On 20th January 1879, the British army set up camp at the base of the isolated, sinister-looking hillock called Isandlwana. They thought it was open high ground which dominated the surroundings, but unbeknown to them there were hidden 'dongas' (dried out watercourses) around the approaches which were invisible from the ground.

On 22nd January, the British army was about to start an invasion of Zululand. A Zulu army of 17,000 men overwhelmed the camp, killing 864 British soldiers and 470 of their African allies. The Zulus suffered about 1,000 casualties. The battlefield is now clearly marked. The nearby small museum has displays of battle dress and memorabilia from both the British and Zulu regiments.

Immediately after this battle, a small British garrison of 139 soldiers based at a mission station at Rorke's Drift was attacked. Two Zulu regiments were sent to pursue refugees from Isandlwana. They were given no instructions to attack the mission station, but were heady with the victory of Isandlwana. About 4,000 Zulus twice attacked the building and later peppered the mission station with bullets. The attack went on until 4am the next day, 23rd January. Dabulamanzi, in charge of the Zulus, realised he had badly exceeded his orders in attacking the building and had already lost 500 men, while 15 British soldiers had been killed and most of the rest injured. The rest of the Zulus withdrew leaving the garrison to attend to its wounded and put out the fires.

Eleven Victoria Crosses were awarded to defenders of Rorke's Drift, the most ever received by a British regiment for a single action.

The last of the Gentleman's Wars

Another historic moment occurred at Spioenkop, although not so rewarding for the British forces. Spioenkop was one of many battles between the Boers and the British in the second Anglo-Boer War of 1899-1902. They called it the last of the Gentleman's Wars.

The Boers were deeply religious, often refusing to attack on the Sabbath. Their leaders were elderly, courteous, well-liked and lacking the killer instinct. The British forces were more used to ceremonial duties, their officers more familiar with lavish ballrooms than the stench of the battlefield.

During the Anglo-Boer War, the British had mounted a hill called Spioenkop. It was very misty and they thought they were at the top of the hill, but they had only reached a plateau. To make matters worse they were overlooked by many Boer positions and artillery. Scouts sent out earlier to reconnoitre the area had seen that this was not a good location from which to fight, being overlooked by other hills. Their messages fell on deaf ears.

When the mist lifted, the British realised they were not atop the hill as they'd thought, and climbed further. As they mounted the top of the hill, the Boers appeared on an adjacent hill and started pounding the British with cannon fire. The British dug themselves in but it was hopeless. Where the Boers missed their target they merely adjusted their sights and then made direct hits upon the struggling British soldiers who were unable to return such fierce fire power. The fighting went on all day.

This battle was significant in that more British soldiers lost their lives in such a small area, in any battle in any war before or since. Official figures put the losses at 300, but unofficially it was nearer 700. Mahatma Gandhi was a stretcher bearer in this battle and Winston Churchill was on hand as a war correspondent for a British newspaper.

Being the height of summer, the weather was hot and the temperature reached nearly 40 degrees. The day after the battle, a trench was dug to bury the bodies of many of those who died that day, as it was impossible to leave bodies for further identification in that intense heat. Others, particularly officers, were buried in single graves. As is traditional in warfare, the Boers did not fight the day after the battle, allowing the British forces to attend to the wounded and bury their dead.

Did you know that Liverpool Football Club's home end is called 'The Kop' because a 'koppie' is a hill and many of the soldiers involved in that battle came from a regiment based in Liverpool? Those that survived took the name back with them to commemorate those who lost their lives at Spioenkop.

The Midlands Meander
Another favourite area of mine is the Midlands Meander. Here, you can drive around small villages

with names like Rosetta, Lidgetton and Nottingham Road and enjoy the scenic countryside.

The area is littered with small art galleries, artisan's studios, exclusive boutiques and coffee shops. There are pottery studios, wood turning studios, metalworkers, art shops and bakeries in a landscape of green rolling hills and waterfalls. Accommodation is provided in quaint guesthouses and thatched cottages with names such as Granny Mouse's Country House. There are many local restaurants in the area offering sumptuous home-made food and wine.

I was particularly impressed by the wood turner's studio with its beautifully made bowls and plates, shining with a high gloss. South Africa has many indigenous trees such as yellowwood, stinkwood and wild pear, with their exotic grains and colours.

I left that studio vowing one day to buy a lathe and learn to turn some pieces of my own. Since then, I have started visiting a hobbies club in Cape Town and in Berkshire where I have had a go with a lathe. At some time in the future I will take this interest more seriously.

... What did I learn?

Be firm with your friend or partner, because they will benefit more than if you are always kind. Don't be afraid to ask for what you want; know what you want and ask for it. Others may see something for themselves in your request, and the result may surprise you.

Chapter 7
The Garden Route Tour

I had been driving for two and a half hours, and it was a relief to see the gate ahead. The temperature was nearly 40 degrees and the cheap hire car did not have air conditioning. I pulled up at the barrier.

Before I could get out, a guard with a clipboard stepped out of his hut.

'Sanbona,' he greeted me with a smile.

'Sanbona,' I answered.

'What's your name, sir?' He checked his list, and I was on it.

'Would you like a cold drink? Pepsi, Sprite, juice?' he asked. What a welcome question! I accepted an apple juice with gratitude.

'You know the way?' he asked next. I shook my head, still gasping from the ice-cold drink.

'No! Is it far?' I asked, as I couldn't see anything in view from where I was sitting.

'Not far,' he said, 'just follow the track and take the right fork about three kilometres down. You'll see the lodge over to your right after about fifteen minutes.'

'Fifteen *minutes*? How far is it?' I asked, realising I still had some distance to go.

'Not far, only about ten kilometres.' He saluted as I drove through the open gate.

Sure enough, about fifteen minutes along the sandy track I came over the hill leaving a dust trail in my wake — and there was the lodge.

As I approached, a lady appeared from the main entrance. She was tall, slim and dark-skinned despite her English appearance. She waited patiently while I negotiated the last few turns. Obviously I was expected.

I stepped out of the car and she removed the car keys that were dangling from my fingers. 'You won't need those for a while,' she smiled. 'Please take the personal bags you need now; the rest of your luggage will be taken to your luxury tent.' She led me into the air-conditioned lodge, a refreshing contrast to the hot and sticky car.

In no time at all I had another cool drink in my hand. I'd arrived!

The welcoming lady introduced herself as Salomé and, once I'd swallowed my drink, she gave me a whistle-stop tour of the lodge and then walked me through to the lawns behind the lodge. A table had been set for lunch.

I was ushered to a chair beside a single table and as I sat in the shade of a tree, with an attentive waiter serving me, I was only thirty metres from a waterhole. Silently drinking from the murky water were several elephants and zebras, and a small family of warthogs.

Every movement of the huge male elephant was audible, as it sucked with its trunk and squirted water over its back. How lucky I was to be in such a beautiful place. And this was my very first experience of animals in South Africa!

I was visiting Addo Elephant Park near Port Elizabeth, having spent two weeks on a business trip driving along the Garden Route from Cape Town. Addo is one of the most important game reserves for the conservation of elephants in South Africa. It is located seventy kilometres north east of Port Elizabeth in the Eastern Cape.

My first game reserve

Gorah is an exclusive game reserve within Addo, and I was privileged to be given a complimentary night's stay there.

I slept in a huge bed in a permanent tent. Inside, it's more like a hotel room than a tent, with its own shower area and his-and-hers basins. My view from the French windows and balcony was of the open grassland, beyond which I could see elephants and buffalo roaming in the distance.

The main building and restaurant area was enclosed by fencing to keep out the dangerous animals. Our accommodation was outside that enclosure, so after dark we had to be escorted to our tent by an armed guard, just in case there was a lion or a leopard lurking. We were more likely to be troubled by the vervet monkeys who had learned that trays of tea and biscuits were left outside on the balcony before breakfast each morning. I had to be quick to fetch it in before it was nabbed by these amiable thieves.

Scary as it was to be escorted to my tent at night, it only heightened my enjoyment to think of the possibility of meeting a dangerous animal on the way.

The evening was spent chatting to my fellow guests around the dinner table, whilst we eagerly tucked into a delicious *cordon bleu* meal immaculately complemented by a bottle of South African wine.

Lonely Valley

A male elephant at Gorah, called 'Valley', had recently arrived from the Kruger Park. Sometimes, if there are too many males in one area, one of them is relocated to keep it safe from the dominant male. Valley was the same age as me at the time, 47. He was 'in musth', as they call it — looking for a mate — but very lonely, and separate from the herd. I remember relating to him a little at the time.

When we encountered Valley we were able to get extremely close, near enough to smell his strong musth and hear every movement of his body. As we sat quietly in the Land Rover, we were instructed to be careful not to startle him. Valley did look like a lonely soul.

Elephants are surprisingly artful creatures. Once, when I was on a game drive in Hluhluwe-Umfolozi Game Reserve, near Durban, we turned a corner and were startled to be confronted by a huge male elephant facing us in the road. It was flapping its huge ears, raising its trunk and trumpeting loudly. I felt a tightening in the pit of my stomach as I had never faced an animal like this before. The road was completely blocked.

As the elephant started to run at us, and initially gained ground, the driver engaged reverse and backed up rapidly. The girls in the back of the vehicle panicked and screamed — and then I noticed the driver smiling. He knew exactly what he was doing.

After we had backed up a little way we stopped in the road and waited for the elephant's next move. This was like a game of chess. The animal stood still and watched us for a while before moving off the road a little to our left. We wanted to go forward and back down this route as the alternative would mean a long detour but this obstacle was directly in our way. We played the waiting game. So did the elephant.

Then it moved towards a tree and hung its trunk casually over a low hanging branch, slightly turning his back to us. The driver waited, and in time decided to pull forward to continue our journey. As we drew level with the elephant, the animal turned sharply and ran at us again. The driver accelerated and soon left the troubled beast behind. It had been a game. The elephant didn't expect to stop us by then but had made its point. *It* was in charge of this territory. Soon we had squeezed by and were gone.

I have seen other elephants push a tree over with a mere flex of their shoulders. There is a huge split and crack as the tree gives in. The animal appears to be able to stretch its neck and shove its shoulders forward whilst its back legs hardly move and its feet stay firmly planted on the ground. What strength!

In certain areas of the landscape you can see where elephants have passed through, stripping trees, ripping branches and tearing bark from the trunk as they sharpen their tusks on the tree.

Seeing the aftermath of an elephant rampage is like following in the wake of a whirlwind. The devastation has become a problem in some areas of the Kruger Park where the herds are large. This is one reason why the groups of elephants are thinned out by culling, or individual animals are relocated.

Elephant surroundings

I had a more frightening experience with elephants while on holiday with my girlfriend in the Kruger Park in 2007.

We were driving out of the park when we came across a herd of elephants visiting a water hole. I counted at least 33 elephants, large and small, as we stopped in a car park overlooking the water hole. We watched a while, as the families of animals entered the water from our left and played the water, leaving to the right of our view. Some were drinking, some were bathing and spraying their backs to keep cool. It was wonderful sight to see so many elephants enjoying themselves at once.

As they left the water on their journey that morning, I suggested to my girlfriend that we back up along the road and watch them cross over. I turned the car around and gently glided in their direction, stopping at what I thought was a safe distance.

It seems that one bull elephant disagreed with me, and took offence. As I kept an eye on it showing its displeasure by flapping its ears, I failed to notice the others coming out of the water and heading in many directions. Suddenly, my girlfriend screamed that a number of elephants were skirting the lake and making for the road behind us. We were being surrounded. I looked left, and sure enough a group of mature beasts were rushing alongside us below, by the water's edge.

As soon as I realised this I put the car into reverse. As I backed up, I realised we were not going fast enough and accelerated harder. There was a moment when I thought we were in trouble — but luck was with us and we managed to escape. All afternoon I tried to understand what these wily elephants had been doing.

Later that week we independently asked two expert guides about this incident. They both assured us that the elephants were probably playing games and perhaps the big male was showing off to the females. If that was true it certainly didn't feel like it at the time!

Tourists playing with fire

As a tourist it's easy to forget how dangerous the animals can be. It may be ignorance or a sense of 'it won't happen to me', but some tourists forget that the land belongs to the animals and we are just visiting.

There is a South African publication called *Getaway* that used to have a regular section using photographs sent in by readers, showing tourists in dangerous locations. Pictures showed people outside their vehicle taking a photograph when very close to wild animals. Some have been known to send their children into the bush, just for a snap of an animal.

The magazine 'named and shamed' the drivers by publishing their vehicle registration numbers. Most of the culprits turned out to be local South Africans who should have known better!

THE TOASTMASTER EXPERIENCE!

Two people had independently suggested I try Toastmasters. Maybe they thought I need to improve my speaking skills. So, I researched the company and found a group near me. They meet twice a month on a Monday evening.

As I sat there on that first visit I was not sure how it would benefit me, yet I wanted to take it further. I had never been good at speaking in public and here was an opportunity to learn some skills.

Toastmasters International is an American based international organisation set up, under different names in different locations, to help people improve their speaking skills in public. There are also opportunities for members to improve their organisational and leadership skills by joining a committee and organising events.

I found the Maidenhead Speakers Club, the group I first joined, to be very professional and full of helpful and supportive people. I was made welcome at the door and someone looked after me throughout that first evening. Every protocol and purpose was explained to me and the other guests that night.

As a new member I was given a manual, as well as introductory leaflets explaining what Toastmaster is about and how I could use the organisation to better myself.

The manual consists of an initial ten speeches, with a set of objectives for each speech such as preparation, clarity of content, body language, vocal variety, speaking with impact and inspirational speaking. I could choose any subject as long as I met the relevant criteria. Each speech builds on the previous speeches.

To help speaking on your feet there is a table topics session each evening where a volunteer has two minutes to speak on a subject revealed only when they are called. So that person has the time it takes to walk from their seat to the front of the room to come up with an entertaining story or speech. It's a difficult thing to do and I made myself get up at subsequent evenings and put myself forward. My first 'off the cuff' speeches weren't very good but it did get me started. It took me many efforts before I felt I had given a satisfactory speech. It has helped me to be a bit quicker responding to everyday events. I think faster now and am more able to come up with a rapid response to a given situation.

The evening itself is very formal and well structured. Everything is timed to keep to a schedule and members are free to take part by choosing any of the roles available during the evening.

Speeches are evaluated by another member so there is always feedback giving people written and verbal comments on their performance. Members are encouraged to be positive and highlight 'areas of improvement' rather than 'mistakes'.

It was a long time before I became confident enough to enjoy standing up there and talking.

Many of the early speeches I heard were well presented, which made me work hard to keep up the good standard of the club. I am still amazed how some people are able to present their first speech without any apparent nerves.

I didn't realise at the time but Toastmasters would help me with guiding. Having presented three speeches by the time, I took my practical exam and had to present a guided tour to my classmates, I was more confident and less nervous than many others in the class that day.

Conversely, guiding also helped with my speeches. Sitting in the front of the minibus talking gave me confidence to stand in front of an audience and tell a story. Straight away I was told at Toastmasters that I had a good conversational manner of speaking—which boosted my confidence no end! I am also accustomed to speaking clearly and slowly, which helps people who are not English-speaking to understand and enjoy their visit better.

The pollination of fynbos

When I was looking for a subject for a speech, the pollination of fynbos came to mind. A guide friend in Cape Town had suggested I choose a subject related to my guiding, so I could prepare a speech and at the same time learn something to enhance my guiding knowledge. What a brilliant idea!

I researched pollination by insects, pollination by birds, pollination by animals and surprisingly pollination by fire.

Insects such as flies and butterflies are attracted to the colourful flowers. A number of plant species rely on one butterfly, the large brown mountain beauty which has a passion for red. The horse fly, the russet fly and the tangle-winged fly have long needle-like mouthparts which suck the nectar from inside the floral tubes. Eight fly species pollinate over eighty different fynbos plant species.

The protea seedeater (canary), Cape siskin, Cape bulbul and red-winged starling all like fynbos, and the sugarbird and the sunbird rely exclusively on fynbos for their survival.

Mice pollinate thirty five species of proteas. The plants flower close to the ground and secrete tasty yeast-smelling nectar to attract the rodent. When the mouse eats the nectar its nose collects the pollen which is then transferred to other plants.

My greatest surprise was to find that fire is essential for fynbos. Many proteas produce seeds that require the intense heat of a fire to regenerate. The plant produces a seed with an oily appendage to attract the harvester ant, which takes the seed into its underground nest and eats the oily appendage, leaving the seed behind. When the next fire passes the seed is stimulated to germinate.

I'd wondered why vegetation sprouts so quickly after a fire. Many fynbos plants protect themselves by burying their stems underground and after a fire they quickly sprout up. Some proteas protect their trunks with a corky insulating bark.

After a fire, the burnt undergrowth provides nutrients for the soil and it is said that for optimum fynbos diversity a fire should take place every 10 to 14 years. Fires appearing too frequently (often by human interference) destroy plants and exhausts seed stocks, resulting in local extinctions.

That was a lot of factual information to learn for a seven-minute speech — and my first one. I still use this information now in some of my guiding. However, I learned to choose less complicated subjects in future.

A history of wine

Another speech I presented was about the wine industry. Did you know that all the wine regions of the world are all within 30 and 50 degrees north and south of the equator? Within these zones the grapes ripen well to make a good wine. In the cool, damp conditions of England and Germany, it is sometimes difficult for the grapes to ripen fully. At the other extreme, hot dry North African countries such as Morocco and Algeria are too hot and insufficient rain leads to overripe grapes with low acidity.

The first wine developments were around the Caspian Sea and in Mesopotamia, near present day Iran. Here, six jars were discovered, one once filled with wine from the kitchen of a Neolithic residence. Patches of a reddish residue were found on the interior of this vessel which is recorded in the Guinness Book of Records as the world's oldest wine jar dating back to before 5000 BC.

The meerkat experience

One of my most amazing animal experiences was being with the meerkats, an experience I shall probably never forget. I used this story as one of my later speeches.

I first met Grant, 'The Meerkat Man' at a tour guide evening in Cape Town in 2006. He gave a fascinating talk on his favourite subject and passion. Meerkats only live in the southern part of southern Africa so we are privileged to see them here.

On a garden route tour the following year, we were up at 4.00 am to meet Grant and the rest of the small group of tourists at a pre-determined location, somewhere outside Oudtshoorn.

We were taken off road in a convoy of cars to the meerkat tunnel site. Only Grant knows where he is going as we set off on foot across the then cool landscape. The animals we are seeking move from one burrow system to another, almost daily so we would find it difficult to see them in the wild.

We stop a few times before we settle at one spot as the sun appears over the horizon, a spot that looks like any other spot on this harsh and dry landscape. "Can you see a burrow?" Grant asked. But there is no reply.

Grant carried on talking and explaining about the life of the meerkat. "They will be up shortly".

Very soon the first meerkat emerged into the sunlight and a broad grin spread across my face. I couldn't believe this was actually happening. This little wild creature was standing about ten metres from me as he checked the surroundings. Grant called him the weatherman; he was also the first lookout. Tomorrow, another animal will probably take his place.

I could see all his features as he stood bolt upright in that now famous 'meerkat pose' with his little paws hanging in front of him, his dark patched eyes noticing everything around him. He sat on his tail leaning back like someone sitting on those sticks at the races. I was fascinated to see the whole body twist, not just his head as the sentry surveyed all around him and gave the all clear. Now a second meerkat had emerged from the burrow. Then, as I learnt from Grant's knowledge, I too could anticipate a third animal appear from his slumber, by the way the sentry moved his head.

They stretch in the sunlight and use the suns rays to heat their little bodies as they all stood together staring at the sun. Apparently, it's not the done thing to stand in their line of the sun. I counted about fourteen meerkats of all ages before they moved off in search of food.

We spent many moments standing in the punishing sun, listening to Grant pour out his knowledge of meerkats, plants and other animals that were all around us. We ate leaves from a salty tasting succulent containing a considerable amount of water. We watched a male spider doing what the larger female expected of him without the knowledge that he will be eaten sometime later.

I may have missed the information about wearing closed shoes as I stamped on the spot to keep the carnivorous ants from crawling over my sandals and up my legs. It was a relief to move on so the flies would stop irritating us too as we followed Grant and the meerkats. But it was worth the inconvenience! Oh it was so worth it!

We walked about two kilometres across the Karoo following these little mites as they burrowed, played, stood watch and fed. It wasn't easy for us as the morning heat became intense and the insects were winning the battle, but it was worth it. Four hours later we were back in our room, showered and tucking into a hearty breakfast and it was still before 10.00 am.

How did this happen? From a background of working with other primates this amazing and dedicated man has spent years studying and recording all aspects of these creatures' behaviour. This is his study group and he knows them well. They all have names and he even knows the date they were born. He doesn't train them as they are still wild, but he has, by repetition and association, got them to realise he is no threat. He makes meerkat noises that make them feel comfortable and over the years he has been able to get closer starting from seeing them at a distance with binoculars to now being able to stand two metres away and talk at normal pitch to us without disturbing them. It was an amazing experience to see this in front of my very eyes.

"It's all about conservation" says Grant. "These animals cannot be kept in zoos and certainly won't be a pet long-term, one of the downsides of the recent television publicity. Meerkats can't be returned to the wild when people are fed up with them as they will die without knowledge of local predators and nearby burrow systems."

Grant is educating farmers that meerkats are good for their farms and not to plough fields which destroy many burrowing animals' habitat. Our visit today supported his cause and proved to the farmer there is another way.

A not so perfect presentation

As a way of maintaining my progress in public speaking whilst overseas, I attend a local club in Cape Town. One day, someone suggested I present the demonstration speech at the local annual competition. The problem was that I would have to face a much larger group — but I would be evaluated by everyone participating in the evaluation contest, so I would get lots of feedback.

The speech I prepared was called 'Love thy fellow man' an inspirational speech that I had drafted almost without the need for editing. It just poured out onto the paper; I was so passionate about it that day. The audience would be about 70 people, larger than I was used to. This in itself didn't daunt me, although I would have to widen my eye contact to accommodate the larger room.

My mistake was to not learn my first lines well enough. I had tried to get the first section of my speech word-perfect, since I felt it would not make sense if I forgot a line. Being so preoccupied about missing anything, I fumbled my early lines, lost a little confidence and then forgot my place.

The presentation gave the competitors something to evaluate instead of trying to find anything to say about a perfect speech. In other respects I carried off the speech well, and it had the thought-provoking impact I wanted.

I repeated the speech at a general evening later that week and won the best speech of the evening award.

At another evening in Cape Town one member asked me if I wanted to be the Toastmaster of the Evening, the member who prepares and presents the evening's event. My first reaction was to say I wasn't ready — but I thought I would be able to achieve it before leaving for the UK some months later. So, that is what I did.

Looking back at how I felt that first evening as a visitor, wondering whether I could be able to run the whole event just 18 months later, I struggled to believe it possible. But, with practice and encouragement from the club, I was able to give a very polished performance as 'Toastmaster of the Evening'. I positively enjoyed doing it, and the audience had a good time. I realised that I can do this sort of thing without difficulty.

Yes, being a member of Toastmasters has helped me a great deal with my guiding.

Back to the Garden Route Tour — Knysna and its lagoon

The Garden Route is considered by many tourists to be the coastal route from Cape Town and Port Elizabeth. Strictly speaking, it really starts at Mossel Bay and extends to a point near Storms River, just past Plettenberg Bay. It is so called because the rain caused by sea evaporation, condensing over the coastal mountain range and watering the area, makes the route so green.

While the whole route is beautiful, there are key areas to see. Places like Mossel Bay, Knysna, Plettenberg Bay and the Tsitsikamma Forest are all worth a visit. George and Oudstshoorn are close by, slightly inland.

Knysna (pronounced Nyze-nah), is a quaint seaside town and one of the most popular tourist destinations in the area.

It is surrounded on one side by forests and on the other by sea, which comes inland through the 'Knysna Heads' and fills the beautiful lagoon, making it an ideal location for family boating and boat trips. A small waterfront containing shops and restaurants stretches into the lagoon, famous for the oysters farmed in its shallow waters.

The views around the area are spectacular and attract many tourists. A one night stopover cannot do it justice. On my first visit, I stayed in one of the many guesthouses up on the hill overlooking the lagoon. It was a steep walk into the town in the evening for dinner but worth the effort. The view of the lagoon from the guesthouse was spectacular.

The Outeniqua Choo Tjoe

I always enjoy a steam train journey and this trip was spectacular. Passing through the beautiful Outeniqua Mountains, the Outeniqua Choo Tjoe was the only steam-hauled scheduled passenger service in the country.

Passengers were mainly tourists. Families, excited children and grandmas filled the carriages to capacity.

Every day, before the winter storms severely damaged the railway infrastructure in August 2006, the train puffed its way from George to Knysna and back, along this part of the Garden Route, passing through spectacular coastal scenery. At one stage, just outside Knysna, the track crossed the bay and there was only water to see when you looked down on either side. Your senses were overloaded as you took in a mixture of fresh sea air and scenery, contrasted with the smell of pine forests and steam, as the engine strained its way up the mountain passes.

The journey took two and a half hours each way, including a short stop at Sedgefield to allow passengers to stock up on drinks or buy an ice cream.

Nowadays, the train has resumed operations between George and Mossel Bay in the other direction, a slightly less spectacular journey in my opinion — but nevertheless exciting for rail enthusiasts and non-enthusiasts alike.

The train is generally hauled by a class 19D or class 24 steam locomotive, with restored carriages that date back to early 1900. The station at George houses the Outeniqua Railway Museum which is well worth a visit.

Along these stretches are the Outeniqua Mountains and the Knysna Forest, which both contain many species of indigenous tree, some of which are not generally found anyway else in the world. The Outeniqua yellowwood is a unique species of the South African yellowwood, used extensively in furniture making and flooring and noted for its straightness and smooth grain.

There is beautiful countryside here and many outdoor activities in the forests. One which I avoid is bungee jumping — including the largest jump in the world, the 216-metre high Bloukrans Bridge, near Storms River.

There are some amazing places to stay in South Africa, many of them located along the Garden Route.

A tree-top experience to remember

One of the most unusual I found was Tsala Treetop Lodge, near Plettenberg Bay. They describe their accommodation as 'a seductive creation of timber, stone, glass and water, built high in the canopy of the indigenous forest overlooking the beautiful Tsitsikamma valley'.

I walked from the car park straight on to an elevated walkway through the trees to inspect one of ten exclusive and very private suites. From six metres up in the canopy, each suite has its own deck and infinity pool. Bathing in this pool, all you see are treetops as you hear the haunting sounds of the forest below. Water pours over one side of the pool into an invisible channel below, giving the illusion of having no side. It is an exceptionally intimate and private location.

This lodge is so, so restful — you can't help relaxing.

Next door to Tsala, and under the same ownership, is Hunter's Country House, an exclusive boutique hotel, offering exemplary service and acclaimed gourmet cuisine. The gracious, original homestead is set in beautiful gardens surrounded by 23 luxurious cottages and suites, each designed for absolute comfort and privacy.

Plettenberg Bay is a beach resort, popular for family holidays. Protected from the open ocean by the spectacular Robberg Peninsula, the bay is an excellent location for sea sport and whale watching. Large seaworthy ski-boats transport visitors into the ocean to see the southern right and humpback whales.

Plett, as it is locally known, is a hive of activity with wonderful beaches for swimming, surfing or just walking.

The Bay of Mussels

Another lovely beach resort which is steeped in history is Mossel Bay. The town has a thriving tourist trade as well as a lovely fishing harbour and museum.

Bartholomew Diaz, the first European to round the Cape, passed here *en route* to the Far East and Spice Islands. Having been at sea for what seemed too long, the sailors threatened to mutiny and Diaz was forced to turn back. He anchored in the bay where he found many mussels, so he named it Mossel Bay. It is very sheltered and early indigenous people lived in the area feeding off the mussels. As a result, large piles of mussel shells were found along the beaches.

The Bartholomew Diaz Museum houses, among other things, a full-sized replica of his ship, a 15th century caravel. Visitors can step aboard and see for themselves what life was like on such a ship. I found it a surprisingly small ship to live on for such a long journey — no wonder the crew nearly mutinied!

Outside the museum is a very old milkwood tree. Once trading started along this route, outward bound sailors would leave a message for their family in this old tree hoping that a returning sailor would take it home and deliver it. The original letter was left in an old boot in the tree, found and delivered to Portugal. Now there is a proper post box by the tree, and visitors can send a message home. The letter will be stamped: 'Posted in the Old Post Office Tree, Mossel Bay.'

The only difference today is that you have to buy a postage stamp!

Ostrich country

Oudtshoorn is a surprisingly different experience. Located inland, just over the spectacular Outeniqua Mountain Pass, Oudtshoorn is the largest town in the Little Karoo. A baby compared to the vast dry semi-desert region of the main Karoo, the town is tucked behind the coastal Outeniqua mountain range. Here, sheep roam the lands and Karoo lamb is, according to South Africans anyway, the best lamb in the world. It is said that the meat tastes of the herbs eaten by the sheep which gives it a distinctive flavour.

Historically, Oudtshoorn is renowned for its commercial success as the centre of the ostrich feather industry and became known as the ostrich feather capital of the world. There are now four ostrich show farms in the Oudtshoorn area where visitors may view the animals in various stages of their growth.

In the surrounding area are many grand buildings left as a result of the success of this commercial town, and the centre is a thriving tourist location. I like how different this area is from the Garden Route — it's only the other side of the mountains yet the scenery is utterly different. The Garden Route can be said to be very 'English' with its green pastures, whereas Little Karoo is dry and scorched from lack of rain.

I heard a story about a boy who lived in Oudtshoorn many years ago. He was frightened by a tremendous noise and objects falling from the sky, so he hid under the kitchen table. He was seven years old, born just after the last rain had fallen in the area. He had never seen rain before, and the weird experience had terrified him.

Just outside Oudtshoorn, the world famous Cango Caves are set deep into the Swartberg mountains. Here, visitors view the finest dripstone caverns, many of which have not been properly explored and are not open to the public.

I took the 'adventure tour', the longer and more adventurous of the two tours available, where we wandered deep into the mountainside through narrow passages with tight bends. At one point my guide told me to climb up a passage they call the chimney, a vertical climb up a tight tube barely wide enough for my shoulders. I thought he was joking, but he wasn't! Once I had ventured in and found a few footholds it became clear that it was possible and finally, exhausted, I crawled out of the top into another fascinating chamber.

The guides permit only people who are of a certain size to take the adventure tour. Apparently, one day a lady insisted that she should be allowed to enter despite the concerns of the staff. She became stuck in the chimney and it took the fire brigade many hours to free her. I think she learned her lesson!

George who?

George is the commercial and agricultural centre of the Garden Route. It is not on the coast and therefore less popular than Plett or Knysna. George has a small but bustling airport which serves the Garden Route towns. It also has magnificent golf courses. The now famous Fancourt is a golf complex with no fewer than four courses, two of which feature in the top ten golf courses in South Africa.

Golf is big business in South Africa and a number of courses are situated along the Garden Route. The courses I have played on have been superb: varied in design and features, a mixture of parkland, heathland and links courses. They are relatively quiet compared with courses in the UK and most are relatively inexpensive.

Other outdoor activities in the area include hiking or walking, canoeing, hang gliding and abseiling. The famous otter trail, a five day walk with accommodation, is so popular that you have to book months in advance. This walk offers some of the most spectacular scenery through the Tsitsikamma Forest. Other walks take in the rugged and breathtaking coastal path along the coast at Storms River.

Most visitors drive the Garden Route in just a few days — yet there is so much to see and enjoy. Some establishments offer a sanctuary away from the busy world outside where visitors can enjoy an atmosphere of relaxation and solitude. It would be a shame to miss this opportunity.

Animal magic

For animal lovers, there are two places worth a visit, both located at the Craggs, near Plettenberg Bay.

The first is the Elephant Sanctuary where you can walk with a rescued elephant into the local forest. I will always remember that the trunk felt wet, yet warm as it nestled in the palm of my hand behind me as the elephant followed me into the forest. I could feel her breathing into my hand and when I turned round her eye and huge head were incredibly close to me. It's awe-inspiring to have such a powerful beast following you like a dog on a lead.

There are regular tours throughout the day, which includes a talk on the habits of an African elephant and an opportunity to touch them. I left knowing that these great animals are very happy in their current environment.

The second visit I enjoyed was to Birds of Eden. Visitors wander through a two-hectare (four-acre) dome over a gorge of indigenous forest where many different species of colourful birds can be viewed. The surroundings are very cool and calming, and we spent hours inside taking countless photographs of these brightly coloured creatures. The amazing colours of the golden pheasant and the absolutely bright red scarlet ibis were a revelation to me, and I was close to many of the colourful Knysna Louries too.

Monkeyland, next door, offers a guided tour through a forest full of a large variety of monkeys.

... What did I learn?

By stretching and testing myself I realise how good I am at new things. I take great satisfaction from achieving new heights, such as a Toastmasters speech — and I would never have found that out if I had not taken those first big steps.

Chapter 8
The Mpumalanga Tour

Mpumalanga (you can pronounce it 'Ma pooma langa') is another of the nine provinces of South Africa and one of the northernmost. It is a wonderful province full of beautiful scenery, culture and wildlife.

The Drakensberg Mountain range extends into Mpumalanga province. On the eastern escarpment of the Transvaal, the lowveld (low pasture) savannah meets the highveld and produces a landscape as hauntingly beautiful as anywhere in Africa.

Over the centuries, rivers have eroded the landscape and created majestic scenery. The Olifants River makes its way down the country through a vast and lovely gorge, leaving red and orange cliff faces from the iron oxides in the water. The Blyde River, a tributary of the Olifants, carves its way seaward leaving a breathtaking valley regarded as one of the scenic wonders of Africa and the third largest canyon in the world.

With a hired car from Johannesburg I set out with my girlfriend to see for myself the beautiful landscape. We spent all day driving around feasting our eyes. With so much to see we could have justified a longer trip. The weather turned misty as the sun started to set. It does rain a lot up there, which is why it's so green.

We based ourselves in Hazyview, very central for the many places to visit in the area. There are good guesthouses and small hotels here, with superb accommodation and a very local welcome. In the shopping centre in Hazyview itself, I felt a little conspicuous amongst so many black South African faces and a little uncomfortable in a world where things are done differently. But I did feel *safe*.

The area around Hazyview is planted with cultivated coconut palms. Beyond this and all around Sabie, there are endless acres of eucalyptus trees grown for the paper industry. The eucalyptus lining both sides of the road is an impressive sight. Often we would meet a huge truck loaded with wood and would have to negotiate our way past as it literally lumbered its way down the valley.

Panoramic Mpumalanga

The Panorama Route is a circular drive around the most spectacular landscape. Robbers Pass is a series of sweeping bends through a beautiful landscape. Highlights include God's Window, the Pinnacle, Wonderview, Bourke's Luck Potholes and Pilgrim's Rest. There are scenic views like that of the Three Rondavels which overlook the Blyde River Canyon. We sat for ages looking at these monsters, wondering how they could have been formed.

The weather changed dramatically and we were pitched into a heavy storm. Thunder and lightning raged around us, as violently as only Africa can muster. It was difficult to drive and I had to slow down to suit the road conditions.

Whilst the roads are generally very good in South Africa, occasionally we came across potholes. There are signs warning drivers of the impending danger and I wonder why they don't repair the roads instead of paying for expensive signs. Perhaps the area is prone to rushes of water from the highlands and the road's sub-base can't cope. Once a hole is repaired another one appears nearby. I had to be alert as some of those potholes would have broken an axle had I hit one!

The rain does provide spectacular waterfalls in the area. In Sabie we walked to the Bridal Veil Falls with water pouring off the cliff like a veil. The walk through the woods was cool and peaceful in the mid-day sun. There are many other waterfalls to see in the area including the Mac-Mac Falls, Horse Shoe Falls and Lone Creek.

Just west of Sabie is the Long Tom Pass which, at 2,149 metres above sea level, is the highest tarred road in South Africa. The pass gets its name from the cannon nicknamed Long Tom by the British and used by the Boers against them in 1900. The pass, built in 1871, is 57 kilometres long with formidable gradients such as the Devil's Knuckles — four consecutive steep summits which became a graveyard for many wagons of that era.

At the confluence of the Blyde and Treur Rivers there was a profitable gold mine known as Bourke's Luck where the rivers converge. Particularly on the Blyde River side, there are extraordinary examples of river erosion known as the Bourke's Luck Potholes. From boardwalks at ground level there are many points to look down and view the circular carvings in the rocks left by countless years of swirling water. There is a pleasant walk from the car park, through the undergrowth and across rocks.

The Gold Rush era

Pilgrim's Rest is now a museum town with only memories of the adventurous, uproarious, naughty and tragic days of old. Its current population of about 1,650 exist to support the museum and restaurants for the pleasure of passing tourists. It is one of the finest examples of a mining town to be seen anywhere in the world.

In 1873 a prospector known as 'Wheelbarrow' Alec Patterson, after his habit of wheeling his belongings in front of him, found alluvial gold (which has been washed downstream by rivers). Another prospector named William Trafford considered he had ended his pilgrimage in search of a fortune and named the valley Pilgrim's Rest.

It wasn't long after the news broke that many other prospectors arrived to seek their fortune, many of these prospectors coming from Britain. A rush took place and by the end of 1875 Pilgrim's Rest boasted twenty one stores, eighteen canteens and three bakeries.

The good thing about having your own car is that you can stay longer. I felt sorry for the people arriving in large buses and small minibuses, to leave after a mere hour or less. We spent hours walking from one museum to the next enjoying the display of old cars, old furniture in a miner's house and the stores with samples of foods available in those days. It was surprising to see brand names on these shelves that would not be out of place in a supermarket of today. Some of the packaging has hardly changed.

Syndicates and large organisations took over the gold extraction in the valley and lone prospectors were eventually lured away to new gold sites. The valley became a profitable gold mining industry for many years with gold extraction continuing in the area until mining ceased there in 1972.

Barberton is another town that grew out of the gold rush. It looked like any other small, yet busy town when we arrived to refresh and refuel — but it has a fascinating history.

The valley became known as the Valley of Death from thick clouds of mosquitoes that haunted the area spreading disease.

In 1884 prospectors, including Graham Barber and his two cousins Fred and Harry, discovered a rift of alluvial gold in the valley, so rich that it glittered. They called it Barber's Reef. It was obvious that a gold rush would occur and a town would develop. The town became known as Barberton, after the cousins, and it grew astonishingly quickly.

Barberton became a place of wild speculation, gambling and fraudulent claims. At the height of its boom the scoundrels and fraudulent companies considerably outnumbered the honest businesses. Some investors made fortunes while many, particularly the British among them, lost heavily.

Initially, Barberton's population consisted of only men with a few fancy ladies arriving later providing well-needed entertainment in the crazy nightlife of a bustling town. One favourite was Cockney Liz, who arrived in Barberton by mail-coach in 1887, apparently in search of her fiancé. She did not find him, but local hotel owner Stafford Parker took her under his wing when he realised that her beauty, combined with her singing and dancing, assured him a full house. She left the town in 1889 having made her fortune.

When the gold was exhausted the town was abandoned. Prospectors turned to Witwatersrand where gold had been discovered, and it eventually made Johannesburg the rich city it is today.

REVIEW

I have not had a real disaster on any of my tours, although I have made mistakes. Tour operators and other tour guides do give good advice — but, as in life itself, the real guiding experience comes from making mistakes.

The first thing I had to learn was the roads to the various hotels in Cape Town. A few are tricky to get to and the correct road is essential. Before I started my full season proper, I decided to cycle around to familiarise myself with them all. Unfortunately, it didn't quite work out that way as other things got in the way.

Initially, I would always memorise the route before leaving the office in the morning — but there would often be a turning I wasn't sure of when I reached it in the minibus. On one occasion I drove around the block three times to find the road into a certain hotel. The passengers in the back didn't notice after the first loop but the next time I had to own up. Another time I couldn't find a hotel and I had to check with the office — only to find it was just a little further up the road. Usually, passengers are still getting to know each other at this stage, and pay little attention to what I am doing.

Initially, I had great trouble getting out of Stellenbosch and finding the correct road to Franschhoek on a winelands tour. The first couple of times I followed my nose and found the right exit. On the point of panic, and about to make an excuse for my error, I suddenly saw the sign we needed. I was very pleased with my sense of direction on those occasions.

Unfortunately, on the next two attempts I failed miserably! That was embarrassing and I swore I would not do it again. I studied the map and drove to Stellenbosch, spending my day off cycling around and learning the route until I felt confident. Now it's easy.

'Make sure when you pick up passengers that they are on the right tour,' I was told by the tour operator. It sounded so obvious yet I did get this wrong once. The worst guiding day I ever had was when I picked up the wrong couple!

I was on a larger minibus seating 19 people that day, and we were going to be nearly full. Stanley was my driver; we had worked together before and got on well.

As we approached the hotel Stanley said: 'I bet that's them,' pointing to two people sitting on a bench. Knowing that Stanley had much more experience than I did, having driven for many years, my judgement was clouded as I asked the couple for their surname and if they were going on a winelands tour. Their name was slightly different to the name on my schedule but started with the same letter. Sometimes the schedule does have the names typed incorrectly, not surprising with so many different foreign names around and the office being busy with bookings at times. However, on the bus, later, I became a little uneasy when they said they were on a full day tour — because I had them scheduled for a half day.

It was as we were making our way to the next pick-up that I asked the couple to confirm their room number, just to be sure. When they gave me a different number to the one on my schedule I knew we had the wrong people, so we turned back.

To make matters worse, I hadn't been to the next guesthouse before, although I knew the area, and I didn't think to ask for clear instructions from Stanley. As I walked past the guesthouse and looked a little lost Stanley came to my aid — all clearly visible from the minibus. As I got back into my seat I wanted the ground to swallow me up. I couldn't wait for the day to end.

Returning to the hotel I quickly found my correct passengers waiting, and assured them we hadn't forgotten them. I also introduced the couple I had picked up by mistake to their frantic guide, strutting around the foyer looking for his missing guests. Luckily both couples were very understanding.

By contrast, one of the other people on the tour made some very derogatory remarks on the feedback form. I'd had no bad comments from the rest of the group so I didn't take it to heart. The day passed off well in the end without further incident and everybody enjoyed their tour.

Although I blamed myself for my error, you have to question why tourists who'd booked a private wine tour with one company would board a nearly-full scheduled bus, having been met by a guide wearing a branded shirt of the wrong tour company. Fortunately I noticed when I did and didn't take them all the way to Stellenbosch!

Many of my early mistakes consisted of missing turnings or not taking the most direct route. Mostly the tourists did not notice.

I found timing and managing the group to be the most difficult task as a tour guide, although I seemed to cope better than many other guides.

People who book private tours with the tour operator are prepared to pay extra so that they don't have to wait while others over stay the agreed time at stops.

On one occasion, a South American gentleman came up to me at Cape Point, having spent time on his mobile phone, and asked how long we had left. Then he disappeared and came back nearly 30 minutes late. The first I knew about it was when others on the minibus said they saw him going up as they were coming down in a hurry to get back. His excuse was that it was such a beautiful location that he wanted to see it properly. I politely made it clear that the others had had to sit in the bus and wait for him and weren't able to see it properly! We were late getting back that evening which made it an even longer day for me.

Earlier, I'd had to ask him to refrain from using his mobile phone on the bus while I was talking. The other passengers later thanked me because it had been annoying them too.

The only other more serious error I made was locking the keys in the minibus. I was returning from a long day's safari, having collected them at six o'clock that morning. We stopped at a trout farm and shop for refreshments. The problem with the particular model of vehicle I was driving is that if you take the keys out and leave the vehicle unlocked, as a security measure it will self-lock after a short delay. I knew this and always kept the keys in my pocket — but on this occasion I was distracted and the doors were closed as the locks shut down.

All the windows were securely closed too and there was no spare key to hand. I had to call the office and they tried to send someone out with a spare key but he was held up in the evening traffic. Eventually they sent out a locksmith with a spare key. This all took nearly two hours to sort out. I was very embarrassed and made great efforts to console the people waiting to go home. In some ways it was fortuitous that I had such a good and understanding group and the hotel next door had a bar. Time seemed to pass quickly for some and one young couple said they enjoyed the drink and chat at the bar. But I felt sorry for a family with two children who I am sure would have preferred to go straight home. In the end I didn't get a single negative report on my feedback forms that day!

I learned early on to make sure my instructions to return were very clear when I had non-English speaking people on the tour. I also learned that some people say yes when they are too embarrassed to admit they don't understand.

These small errors are dwarfed by the countless successful tours I have guided. Many tourists have left South Africa having had a wonderful time as a result of my guiding. I always put a lot into each tour to ensure clients have a great experience, and I will continue to do so as long as I am a guide.

The present

Now I walk along the street with my head held high. I mean that literally. I have more confidence now and a better sense of self-worth.

I am a very different person to who I was just a few years ago.

Also, I have achieved something real. Having been involved with God's Golden Acre I have been able to help people less fortunate than myself, and it feels good. My contribution is on a small scale compared with other people's achievements, such as Heather Reynolds, yet I will probably never know the true worth of my efforts as it will spread far and wide.

To date I have inspired five groups to fly to South Africa to build a house for someone who needs one. Another group is now in the making. The volunteers in those groups will benefit, and so will the people they are helping. There is no reason why this couldn't continue for the foreseeable future.

The world is a slightly better place for me being here. After all, isn't that why we are on this planet? Isn't it our purpose in life, to love and to make a difference?

This story is how I changed my lifestyle and outlook on life. I have given myself a purpose and a direction rather than just to go with the flow as I used to.

I chose to use self development as a vehicle for transforming myself and attended many courses, but I had to do it myself. Nobody could do that for me.

Sitting in that seminar, that first evening, I was struck by how self-expressed many people were, how willing to stand up and tell their story. It would be a bonus if I could achieve half of the confidence they had, I remember saying to myself. Well, I have achieved that and much besides. I now have a story to tell and I have made a significant contribution by supporting another community like GGA.

Others may feel differently about the route I took — it's not for them. I believe there is something for everyone who is prepared to look at themselves and ask: *where can I improve myself? How can I be a better person?*

My mother asks why things always work out for me and not so for others. My answer is that I make them work. I believe passionately in what I do, and that inspires people around me to help and support me.

My father says I am uplifting. I encourage him to do the things he wants to do rather than just finding obstacles.

My 92-year-old girlfriend!

I am told I give a lot to people. At the end of the Tony Robbins seminar, the subject was *contribution*. We each made a promise to go home after the weekend and give our time to an elderly person. If all 9,000 of us did that, it would represent a huge amount of contribution.

Remembering the nursing home in my village, the one where I had organised a garden party a few years ago, I arranged to meet the lady in charge. When I eventually did, I explained that I wanted to spend some time with a resident who might not have regular visitors. She told me it would be against health and safety regulations to allow a stranger into a room with a resident. I wouldn't be allowed.

I left disappointed. And then I realised that I already knew a lady who had offered her help with the garden party.

Sybil lived in Twyford all of her life and her father and grandfather built most of the houses in the area. She was a very popular person who has given much to the local community. She started the local amateur dramatics society and had twice persuaded me to help out at the annual pantomime. She started playing the church organ at the age of 16 and continued playing every Sunday, often more than one service a day, for 68 years. Even at 92 years old, Sybil still had her faculties. She had been unable to play piano for our garden party but offered her support in other ways.

When I returned a tape recorder she lent me a few days later, she asked: 'Can I keep in touch with you? You have done such a wonderful thing for these people and I would like to hear more about you.' I mentioned that I was leaving soon for my six-month world tour so that would be difficult for a while. 'How fascinating,' she said. 'Send me your new address.'

'I will be travelling a lot,' I said, 'but I have set up my parents with an e-mail address so they can keep in touch.' But Sybil didn't have a computer.

As I had only met her twice, it was with some surprise that some weeks later in far off South America I received an email from Sybil. A friend had agreed to send a message on her behalf. Her friend would visit every Thursday and read her my emails, and over that period Sybil sent me the odd letter which was typed into an email by her friend. I was astounded that she made that effort and also a little flattered. She even bought a world map to track my travels and follow where I had been.

When I returned, Sybil proudly showed me the file containing every email I had sent her.

Sybil turned out to be a wonderful friend so it was quite apt that I should offer *her* my time. It was the least I could do. Also, Sybil has given so much to others over her long life that I decided it was time for me to offer something to her in her later years. At the time she had recently lost someone dear to her who would have cared for her. She felt lost without him. I would not be able to replace that person, but at least I could be there for her sometimes.

Over the years I have given her hope and made her day with my visits. When she was very ill I was unfortunately away in South Africa and she didn't expect to see me again. After her illness she was wheelchair bound and I took her out into the garden and down the street. She started to desire greater things and believed she could get better. We went to church together one Sunday which she enjoyed immensely. Others took her on subsequent Sundays. It was these trips out that gave her hope and encouraged her to believe she had a future.

I enjoyed her company as she had such a young active mind. She inspired me too and gave me ideas for my plans. We both got a lot out of each other. I got so much from visiting her and seeing that I brightened up her day. The fact that my visit was so welcomed by Sybil made the small effort worthwhile.

Sadly, Sybil passed away in January 2008, a great loss to her family, friends and the local community alike.

I have no regrets about the efforts I have made to better myself, nor the expense of it all. Sometimes you have to take a risk. Sometimes 'you have to speculate to accumulate'. Each year I treat myself to a course to further my self-development and to stretch myself, like a good entrepreneur would do to improve his or her business skills. This is my business!

Back to the Mpumalanga Tour — singing and dancing, Shangaan style!

One evening we visited the Shangana Cultural Village. Here we were entertained with a dinner and a live performance of dance and song, all set around the story of the villagers' past. A guided tour of the village taught us about their housing layout and marriage arrangements. Their singing is rich with harmonies, and it was easy to understand the story of their history in their dancing.

The first course consisted of barbecued meat served on a platter just after we arrived. Later, after the dancing, we moved inside and sat in a 'rondavel' (a round hut) with the food displayed in the centre. We were first offered a bowl of warm water and a towel to wash our hands. After receiving a plate we were free to help ourselves to the delicious food. The food was very good with lots of vegetable dishes.

Served from iron pots, we sampled beef stew, baked butternut, honey-glazed sweet potatoes and wild spinach with peanuts, all served with freshly baked maize bread. I will never get used to their traditional dishes like mieliepap (boiled flour and water) and samp (a coarse porridge of crushed corn kernels). Dessert was a delicious selection of fresh fruit.

Golf, anyone?

Here's a surprise: you can play golf in the Kruger Park! The course is just outside Skukusa, which is a centre for camping-style family holidays. The accommodation seemed basic after the luxury we had been getting used to, especially the previous night, but we accepted it as we were able to play golf nearby.

The course is a nine-hole public course, independent of Skukusa Camp. The people in the pro-shop could not be more friendly. Normally, when I arrive at a new golf course, I enquire about any local rules, expecting to hear about out-of-bounds on the first hole or some such thing.

We were told: 'If you see an elephant or a lion, just stand still!'

Playing golf in the Kruger is amazing. There are so many colourful birds, and the sounds are totally different from what I am used to when playing my favourite sport at home.

The first hole is alongside a lake. When I was on the putting green, the yawning of the resident hippo disturbed me — although not enough to make me miss my shot.

As we approached the third tee, baboons and impala moved away into the undergrowth. I was slightly concerned about our cameras and other belongings, with baboons around, but these animals were more frightened of us than their brethren in the Cape had been.

On the fifth hole, we found a warthog family on the green. As we approached, they continued munching on the grass, slowly moving away to the safety of the nearby trees.

A ball of a different kind

We also saw a dung beetle pushing a ball of dung to a nest nearby. This species collects animal dung and rolls it into a ball for easy transport to the nest. The female lays her eggs inside. Other species of dung beetle lay eggs directly into the dung, but these are less successful as many piles of dung are found on roads and are often flattened by passing motorists.

The beetle rolls with its hind legs, its head on the floor so it can't see where it's going. Every now and then the beetle stops rolling its ball and climbs on top, turns in a full circle to check its direction, and then climbs down to continue on its way.

An interesting find at Skukusa is the Selati Train Restaurant and Museum. Selati was the destination of the train from Komatipoort. In 1880, a rumour that gold had been discovered in the Selati River Gold Field, near Leydsdorp, sparked one of the biggest railway scandals of the day. The Baron Oppenheim and his brother floated the 'Selati Railway Company' to build a railway line from Komatipoort to the 'new Transvaal gold field' on the Selati River. Some 80 kilometres of track from Komatipoort to Skukusa were laid before anyone had verified that the gold find was genuine. After Shukusa, came the Sabie River, but then the money ran out before a bridge over the river was attempted and the company crashed owing its creditors 800,000 rand. This section of railway is considered one of the most expensive railways ever built.

The restaurant is situated on the old station platform, full of railway memorabilia. An old steam train stands beside the platform and the last carriage has been tastefully converted into a bar. Diners sit at tables spread along the platform and are served by waiters and waitresses wearing navy overalls as if they were stoking the engines.

The birds of the Kruger Park

I have never been in a place bursting with so many different types of pretty birds.

A common bird to this area is the lilac-breasted roller. There are many other rollers too, and when they fly all you see is a flash of various shades of blue. The common bee-eater is another colourful bird with its black and white mask, reddish-brown plumage and bright blue lower tail feathers. The hornbill with its large curved beak is a distinctive shape in flight. One of the reddest birds I have ever seen is the southern red bishop. The male is almost entirely red with a black face and black chest.

The most striking bird is the African hoopoe, with its cinnamon-coloured body black-tipped crest and black and white wings. Alongside the rivers you can readily spot one of the many species of kingfisher family.

The oxpecker is often seen clinging to the neck of a buffalo, rhino or hippo. This bird is accepted by the animal it befriends as it cleans the beast of irritating flies. It's interesting to see how these different animal and bird species live in harmony in the wild, each helping the other.

The francolin, a ground feeding bird not unlike a partridge, is a common sight in the Kruger. There is also the Cape francolin which you see around Cape Town.

Sometimes there are many eagles together, and often a number of them in the sky. With so many carcasses around it's not surprising to see so many birds of prey.

My favourite bird was the paradise whydah with its long broad black tail. It looks tail-heavy when it flies, as it climbs and dips like a train at an amusement park.

Back in Cape Town, an amusing — sometimes annoying — bird is the hadeda ibis. It is the grey-black cousin of the black and white sacred ibis and is often seen in private gardens searching for worms. They irritate me with their wailing cry. A local joke is that they can't stand heights so when they fly they wail as if scared.

I have already mentioned the European birds that have been imported to South Africa such as the house sparrow, the European starling and the chaffinch. Any indigenous birds from the same family seem to be far more colourful in South Africa. Take the red–winged starling. Unlike the European starling, this bird is a bright shiny black with red flashes on its wings which are very noticeable in flight. These birds are a nuisance at camp sites and open restaurants where they congregate looking for food.

... What did I learn — and what's in it for you?

Ask the right question and you'll get the right answer. 'How can I be a better person?' is a good question.

Give your time to someone who is elderly or lonely. You will be surprised what you will get out of it. It's a win–win deal.

Epilogue

Today, I am a different person.

When I left for that trip around the world in 2001, I could feel each day the benefit I had gained from the work I've carried out on myself and from the courses I'd attended. After a while, I stopped noticing the difference — I had become used to it. I now cannot remember exactly how I used to be.

Whenever I would board a crowded train, and saw one solitary seat in the middle of a row of three, I would rather stand in the crowded aisle than disrupt the people around that seat. Now, if there is a seat, I will go and get it, considerately of course! There were many times when I would live my life by thinking of others too much. These days I consider myself more. That is not selfishness — just honouring myself.

A small point, but nevertheless a valuable one: when you stop worrying about yourself and what others think, you free up a lot of brain space for something more valuable.

Whilst the brain has a huge capacity, our 'used' brain capacity is finite. The more we clog it with worries, the less capacity we have for important things. People will have some opinion of you anyway, regardless of your actions, because that is what humans do. So, don't worry!

Control your thoughts and you take control of your life. It's more than positive thinking. I believe you are what you think! If you think things will go wrong they probably will. It's all down to your focus. When things aren't working out, maybe you should change your focus and concentrate your imagination on a positive outcome. It may surprise you how often this works.

Positive thoughts cause endorphins to flow through the body which creates physical pleasure, works towards the healing of wounded and diseased tissues, and boosts the immune system. This in turn helps to improve vitality and a sense of wellbeing. More on this interesting subject can be found in The Endorphin Effect by William Bloom.

Things do go wrong. It's pointless aiming for a perfect world. Life isn't like that. The universe has a way of creating balance and it happens in nature all the time. There must be bad along with good, rich with poor, disasters with miracles. Don't fight it — embrace it. Living will become a lot easier.

Physically handicapped people are rich in many other ways. Some have particular talents that others can only dream of. And do they complain?

When things do go wrong, rather than feel like the victim, why not look for the good in the situation? It is there if you look for it. Put things in perspective — is it really that bad? Is it life-threatening? Sometimes, relating our little problem to those of a friend who is seriously ill can make our problem seem trivial. I may get frustrated when something else goes wrong, but then I see it as a challenge to overcome. In the end, it will make me a better person.

Asking the right question will astound you! I often use the technique of asking myself a question before retiring to bed, and finding that the answer pops up in the morning. This happens because the brain works on the answer while we are asleep. But we have to ask the right question!

Aim high. If you are going to have a dream, make it a big one. You don't have to limit yourself to the feats of others. Be extraordinary. One of my favourite phrases is: 'It is better to aim high and fail than to aim too low and not realise your true potential'. We are so conditioned by our parents, schools and others that failure is a bad thing, we become afraid to stretch ourselves and try something new. When you learn from the experience, rather than labelling it a mistake, anything is possible.

Live life as if 'anything is possible' and extraordinary things will happen. This is an amazing place to be. Life takes on a new meaning when you stop thinking 'it didn't work last time' or 'I might upset them if I call now'. The next time is always a different set of circumstances — the outcome is not a forgone conclusion. It's surprising how much you get done in a short space of time too.

Trust your instincts: they are nearly never wrong! It takes confidence to know your instincts but once you master it you will rarely make mistakes. On a few occasions I have overruled my instincts and have paid the cost.

You don't have to feel ready to be ready. As a perfectionist, I always want to have it all complete before I feel ready — but I have realised I can do things without being ready. So don't wait. Do it anyway!

Nowadays I have a different relationship with strangers. I have learnt to 'love' everyone. Rather than doing what I always used to do, and forming my own opinion, I see them for what they are. We all form a first impression of a stranger, which immediately labels them, based on our previous experience. This means we 'filter' everything that person says and does into our known way of listening. The result is that we are not open to new ideas and opportunities.

Once upon a time I had fixed ideas about people based on their looks, their size and their accent. This view would reflect in my face and body language in some way and the stranger would react accordingly — usually defensively. We are not always aware of this happening. Today, I have learnt to be open and to enjoy their company. This results in us both having a better relationship, even if only for a short meeting.

I love meeting people because I learn from them. Every contact is an opportunity, and I always learn something from that initial encounter. Travelling on my own, I'll often speak to someone in the airport check-in queue, for example. If it turns out that they have already been to where I am going, then I benefit from that conversation. Isn't it better to strike up a conversation with a stranger and learn something, rather than both waste time forming an unrealistic opinion based on incorrect and out of date data?

When I want advice I speak only to experts. There are many well-meaning friends and self-proclaimed experts out there but very few truly know everything about the subject. My father used to get in a terrible muddle over this. Once, he wanted to buy a camera and asked all his friends what to do. Not surprisingly, he received lots of different advice and was left with a dilemma. Which was the correct advice?

There are few true experts out there. Depending on the seriousness of the knowledge I seek, it may cost me money to get it. You could even go to the world's greatest expert in their field if you had to! Sometimes there is no short cut or cheap option. It may take time and research.

Get into action. Don't just think about it. Step out of your comfort zone, stretch yourself and you will be surprised by what you can achieve.

Contribution is the missing link. Whether it's a continuous financial contribution or the time you give willingly, the wealth you create from your actions will benefit many people — and you will find it rewarding too.

And finally, I have a request.

Now you have taken the time to read this book, I ask you to spare another hour and visit an elderly or lonely person and give them your time and attention. We can all think of someone who could benefit from our effort, if only we made the time.

Please, make a promise and make someone happy today.

Appendix

Landmark Education
163 Eversholt Street
London
NW1 1BU
Telephone: 020 7969 2020
www.landmarkeducation.com

God's Golden Acre, UK
Marriage Hill Farm
Bidford on Avon
Warwickshire
B50 4EP
Telephone: 01789 772409
www.godsgoldenacre.org.uk

www.homesofhope.org.uk

Tony Robbins
www.tonyrobbins.com

Happy House
Laimbach 7
3663 Laimbach
Austria
Telephone: 00 43 275 85005
www.tonyandnickivee.com
email: info@tonyandnickivee.com

Grant M. McIlrath
A.K.A. The Meerkat Man
Telephone: 00 27 44 272 3077
www.meerkatmagic.com
email: gmmcilrath@mweb.co.za

Further Reading

1. Just Nuisance AB - His Full Story
   Terrance Sisson
   Published by Flesch Publications
   ISBN 094998938X

2. God's Golden Acre: A Biography of
   Heather Reynolds
   Dale le Vack
   Published by Kregel Publications
   ISBN 1-85424-706-9

3. Echoes of Slavery: Voices from South
   Africa's Past
   Jackie Loos
   Published by New Africa Books
   ISBN 0 86486 661 5

4. Notes from a Friend
   Anthony Robbins
   Published by Pocket Books
   ISBN 0-7434-0937-X

5. The Endorphin Effect: A breakthrough
   strategy for holistic health and spiritual
   wellbeing
   William Bloom
   Published by Piatkus Books
   ISBN 0-7499-2158-7

6. Follow Your Heart: Finding Purpose in
   Your Life and Work
   Andrew Matthews
   Published by Seashell Publishers
   ISBN 0-6463-1066-6

7. The Richest Man in Babylon
   George S Clason
   Published by Signet/New American
   ISBN 0-4512-0536-7

8. The Monk Who Sold His Ferrari
   Robin S Sharma
   Published by Element Books
   ISBN 978-0-0071-7973-2

9. Rich Dad, Poor Dad
   Robert Kiyosaki
   Published by Little, Brown Book Group
   ISBN 0-7515-3271-1

10. The One Minute Millionaire:
    The Enlightened Way to Wealth
    Mark Victor Hansen and Robert G Allen
    Published by Vermilion
    ISBN 0-0918-8463-2

Printed in the United Kingdom by
Lightning Source UK Ltd., Milton Keynes
141042UK00001B/2/P

9 781438 943435